Praise for *He Asked For It*

"*He Asked for It* is a virally gay-centric play, very out there, and sometimes an eye-opener in its frankness and language. Despite the heated sex talk, unbelievable but apparently true practices, and porn-bespattered dialogue, its shock value is in the realization that rather than merely casual sex, most wish lists include a universal desire for identity, acceptance, and connection... Patterson's world premiere play is funny, wicked, and a bit shocking, moving quickly from comedy to drama."
—Madeleine Shaner, *Back Stage West*

"Patterson has accomplished quite a feat in writing a play that tackles tough issues around HIV while getting his audience to intermittently roar with laughter. Even though this play is nothing like *Angels in America*, I daresay that Mr. Kushner would be proud."
—Amita Parashar, *The Advocate*

"Love and loss in Los Angeles are beautifully portrayed in Erik Patterson's seriocomic play."
—*Hotter In Hollywood*

"Frequent flashes of potent behavioral truth... Patterson's brightest gifts—authentic idiom, sharp humor, beautifully layered dialogue—are on display... This is a brave, worthy take on a difficult topic."
—David C. Nichols, *Los Angeles Times*

"The show is really a treat: sexy, provocative, controversial and hilarious to boot... brave and brazen."
—Kiff Scholl, *BeOneCity.com*

"A remarkably insightful view of urban gay life in the 21st century... A work with universal themes about loneliness in the big city and the fragility of the human heart."
—*Frontiers Magazine*

"An amazing play... A phenomenal play... It was funny and sexy and dirty and smart and hilarious and sad and painful and thought-provoking and amazingly moving...I walked out of *He Asked for It* and into the cold rain simply thrilled with the whole experience. As I drove home, I said to myself, 'This is why actors need to do really great theatre. This is why casting directors need to get their asses out there and see really great theatre.'"

—Bonnie Gillespie, *showfax.com*

"Writer Erik Patterson has written an AIDS play with a difference. His take on the subject is fresh, provocative and unpredictable, his characters are engagingly human, and he finds plenty of comedy along the way."

—Neal Weaver, *LA Weekly*

"Gay-themed dramas charting thematic territory that feels truly new are rare, and those that pack a knockout dramatic punch are even harder to come by... Erik Patterson's gripping and intelligent new play feels like a watershed piece. This is a frank and eye-opening view of contemporary urban gay culture that's hard-hitting without being exploitative. It's as funny as it is tragic, eloquently reflecting the bittersweet contradictions of life... This is a vital new work."

—Les Spindle, *IN LA Magazine*

He Asked For It

Plays by Erik Patterson

Tonseisha

Yellow Flesh / Alabaster Rose

Red Light, Green Light

He Asked For It

Sick

I Wanna Hold Your Hand

One of the Nice Ones

Handjob

Books by Erik Patterson

Pop Prompts: 200 Writing Prompts Inspired by Popular Music

Pop Prompts For Swifties: 99 Writing Prompts

He Asked For It

by Erik Patterson

Camden High Street Books
2023

He Asked For It is copyright © 2023 by Erik Patterson

He Asked For It is published by Camden High Street Books

All rights reserved. Except for brief passages quoted in newspaper, magazine, radio or television reviews, no part of this book may be reproduced in any form or by any means, electronic or mechanical, including photocopying or recording, or by an information storage and retrieval system, without permission in writing from the publisher.

Professionals and amateurs are hereby warned that this material, being fully protected under the Copyright Laws of the United States of America and all other countries of the Berne and Universal Copyright Conventions, is subject to a royalty. All rights, including but not limited to, professional, amateur, recording, motion picture, recitation, lecturing, public reading, radio and television broadcasting, and the rights of translation into foreign languages, are expressly reserved. Particular emphasis is placed on the question of readings and all uses of this book by educational institutions, permission for which must be secured from the publisher: camdenhighstreetbooks@gmail.com.

Performance Licensing and Royalty Payments. Amateur and professional performance rights to this Play are strictly reserved. No amateur or professional production groups or individuals may perform this Play without obtaining advance written permission. Required royalty fees must be paid every time the Play is performed before any audience, whether or not it is presented for profit and whether or not admission is charged. All licensing requests and inquiries concerning amateur and professional performance rights should be addressed to the author at erik@erikpatterson.org.

Print ISBN: 978-1-7379853-8-9
eBook ISBN: 979-8-9878016-5-9

Library of Congress Control Number: 2023902514

First Paperback Edition, March 2023

Copy editing by Sherry Angel
Cover image by gryffyn m on Unsplash

Printed in the United States of America
Los Angeles, CA
www.erikpatterson.org

"But better die than live mechanically a life that is a repetition of repetitions."
—D.H. Lawrence, *Women in Love*

PRODUCTION HISTORY

He Asked For It had its world premiere at Theatre of NOTE in Los Angeles on April 25, 2008. It was directed by Neil H. Weiss. The scenic design was by Carlos Moore, the lighting design was by Michael Montenegro, the sound design was by Dennis Yen, the original music was by John Ballinger, the costume design was by Tye Olsen, the production stage manager was Jenna Banko, and it was produced by David Bickford, Lisa Kenner, and Reena Dutt. The cast was:

TED/HOLLYWOODTED	Joe Egender
NEAL/FUNSPORT9	Brad C. Light
RIGBY/RIGBYINLA	Christopher Neiman
MARCUS	Joel Scher
SOPHIE	Rebecca Sigl
HENRY/LOOKINGFORTHEONE	Ron Morehouse
STEVE	Joe Roche

He Asked For It was subsequently produced in Los Angeles with Eleven Eleven Productions, in association with Macha Theatre/Films and Lisa Kenner, opening on June 12, 2009. It was directed by Neil H. Weiss. The scenic and lighting design was by Jeff McLaughlin, the sound design was by Cricket Myers, the original music was by John Ballinger, the costume design was by Jamie Hebert, the projection design was by Thomas Ontiveros, the casting was by Paul Ruddy, and the production stage manager was Jenn Banko. The cast was:

TED/HOLLYWOODTED	Joe Egender
NEAL/FUNSPORT9	Carter MacIntyre
RIGBY/RIGBYINLA	Andrew Keegan
MARCUS	Brian Unger
SOPHIE	Sarah Foret
HENRY/LOOKINGFORTHEONE	Jeremy Glazer
STEVE	Kyle Jordan

The understudies were Alex Boling, Ber Fox, Nathan Frizzell, Brian Guest, Sean Hemeon, and Lisa Schwartz.

SETTING

West Hollywood. Early 2000s.

Los Angeles is a diverse city and the casting must reflect that.

CHARACTERS

TED, 20s, an actor from Wyoming.

NEAL, 20s, a buff, gym dude.

RIGBY, 40s, a gaffer from Encino.

MARCUS, 50s, Ted's agent.

SOPHIE, 16, Ted's sister.

HENRY, 30s, not an actor, a romantic.

STEVE, 20s, an athletic stud.

NOTES

The dialogue should move at a clipped pace, only taking "beats" when indicated. A right slash indicates an overlapping in dialogue. Words in brackets [like these] are thought, but not said.

When actors are engaged in IM conversations, they mime the act of typing, while speaking out. They should not have eye contact with each other during IM conversations. Same rules apply with telephone conversations. We should feel the distance created by these devices.

Since *He Asked For It* was originally produced in 2008, I've written a new third act. The actor who plays Ted should also play Ethan in this new Act Three.

ACT ONE

SCENE ONE

2004.

Crunch Gym in West Hollywood.

Neal runs on a treadmill, reading Us Weekly. *Ted enters. He runs on the treadmill next to Neal.*

After a beat, Ted checks Neal out. Neal catches Ted looking at him. Ted looks away. Neal checks Ted out, isn't interested, goes back to his magazine. Ted looks back at Neal. Neal catches Ted looking at him again. Ted nods at Neal and smiles. Neal politely nods back.

TED: I'm Ted.
NEAL: Neal.

Neal returns his attention to his magazine. Beat.

TED: Can I...uh...I mean, do you...um...

NEAL: You wanna ask me something?

TED: Do you like Madonna?

NEAL: That's what you wanna know about me?

TED: Do you like her music?

NEAL: Random.

TED: Is it?

NEAL: Yeah.

    No.

TED: No, it's not random?

NEAL: No, I don't like her music. That's all you wanna know?

TED: No—okay—sorry—wait—yeah—another question.

NEAL: Shoot.

TED: Do you have a girlfriend?

NEAL: I thought you were flirting with me.

Neal speeds up his run. Ted tries to match him.

TED: I was. I mean, I am. Sorry, I moved to LA three weeks ago. Where I grew up, everyone has a girlfriend. I mean, everyone swings that way, if you know what I mean. I mean—at least, everyone I knew. I'm sure there were other guys—like me—who didn't have girlfriends, but I was never any good at finding them. Then when I went to college, there were some guys there who didn't have girlfriends, if you know what I mean. I mean, do you know what I mean? I keep saying "I mean." Oh my God. What am I trying to say? This is painful. Anyway, fast forward. Or rewind. Or whatever—let me start over: I was trying to figure out if you were...*you know*. Which is ridiculous, because I'm—you know—but I never got that radar thing we're, like, supposed to get. So I'll just ask you again: do you have a girlfriend, and if you don't, then, do you, like, have a boyfriend?

NEAL: No.

TED: But you are, um...

> *Neal waits a beat to see if Ted can say the word.*

NEAL: ...I am.

TED: Sometimes I wish everyone had to wear tags.

NEAL: Tags?

TED: So there was never any question. You could just look at someone and you'd immediately know what they were from their tags.

NEAL: That sounds awful—

TED: No, you don't understand, I mean, then it wouldn't be an issue anymore. Sexuality. It'd be something like hair color or eye color—

NEAL: It *is* something like hair color or eye color—

TED: But you know what I mean—it'd be something you knew immediately—

NEAL: You're proposing a Nazi state.

TED: I'm not making myself clear—I'm just saying that I wish there wasn't so much guessing involved. I'm always guessing if someone *is* or *isn't*. And I wish I just knew. I wish no one had to pretend. Anywhere. Pretend they weren't...*you know*.

> *Neal stops his treadmill. Gets ready to go.*

NEAL: It might help if you could actually say the word.
TED: It's hard to meet people, that's all.
NEAL: You should try the internet.
TED: I'm afraid of the internet.
NEAL: *Dude*. The internet.
TED: Actually...
   I was wondering if maybe you'd wanna go out. With me?
NEAL: Sorry, but I don't go out with guys I meet at the gym.

> *As Neal exits...*

TED: Oh, okay. I can respect that.

> *Ted stands there, alone.*

> *Lights shift.*

SCENE TWO

Basix Café, 3 weeks later.

Ted stands at the bar, dressed for a date.

Rigby enters.

RIGBY: Excuse me, are you—
TED: I'm Ted. / You're Rigby?
RIGBY: I'm Rigby.
TED: Nice to meet you.

They shake hands. Check each other out.

I gave them my name. It'll be about ten minutes. How'd you know who I was?
RIGBY: I recognized you from your profile.
TED: I've never met anyone from the internet before. I'm a little bit nervous.
RIGBY: Don't be.
TED: I read your profile ten times.
RIGBY: You're exaggerating.
TED: I don't exaggerate. I'm not an exaggerator.
RIGBY: Ten times?
TED: Ten times.

RIGBY: Was that before you emailed me or after?

TED: Five before and five after.

RIGBY: Five before and five after, that's—

TED: It's kind of—

RIGBY: It's obsessive.

TED: Or thorough.

RIGBY: I don't know if I should be scared or flattered.

TED: You should be flattered. It was well written. It made me want to meet you.

RIGBY: How's the real thing compared to the profile?

TED: It's good. You're good.

Beat.

How about me? Do you like me? I mean, we met two minutes ago, but is your first impression—

RIGBY: It's good.

TED: You're sure?

RIGBY: I'm positive.

TED: It's surreal meeting a guy from the internet—because I feel like we know so much about each other, but we really don't know anything.

Beat.

I'm not perfect, you know.

RIGBY: That's fine. I'm not either.

TED: I don't understand guys who want perfection. I mean, who's perfect, right? Oh, and this might be a weird question, but I have to ask if you're out of the closet?

RIGBY: I'm forty-five years old.

TED: Is that a yes?

RIGBY: There comes a point in your life when, if people don't like who you are, you gotta just tell them to fuck off, you know? Anyway, yeah, I'm out of the closet.

TED: It's just that everyone I've ever dated was in the closet and I vowed I'd never put myself in that position again. It was too stressful. So I had to ask.

RIGBY: You're not from LA.

TED: No. I grew up in Casper, Wyoming. If you wrote "WYOMING" across the state, Casper's where the "M" would be. It's a big city by Wyoming standards, but compared to here it's practically a ghost town. Which is obviously appropriate because of the name. All the guys I've ever dated—the closeted guys—that was in Casper.

RIGBY: Are you out with your family? In Casper, Wyoming.

TED: Well, I wasn't, and then I was. And that was *different*. My parents, they...they don't really...I mean, are you close to your parents?

RIGBY: No.

TED: Right. Well, I was. So, yeah. Anyway—I moved to LA, and here I am, and...I wanna find someone who isn't afraid to be real.

RIGBY: You moved to Los Angeles to find someone who isn't afraid to be real?

TED: Funny, I know. It's just that...I know I'm young, and I know I'm naïve, but...I want the long haul, I wanna have something with someone that's totally unlike anything anyone else has ever had with anyone else—a completely unique connection. With someone I can be vulnerable with, and human with, and not-perfect with. And this other guy—he doesn't have to be perfect either, as long as we're not perfect together.

RIGBY: Are you for real?

TED: Yeah.

RIGBY: I don't know that I've ever met anyone like you.

TED: Is that a good thing?

RIGBY: Definitely. And today's your lucky day, because if you want real, I can be real.

TED: Really? Then tell me something "real" that's not in your profile. Something most people don't know about you.

RIGBY: This is embarrassing, but...

TED: Tell me—

RIGBY: I cry a lot. It just happens. It doesn't even necessarily mean I'm sad or happy. I'll just cry.

TED: How often?

RIGBY: Every day.

TED: You're making this up—

RIGBY: It usually happens when I'm in the car—alone. I don't know why that is.

TED: You just cry?

RIGBY: That's something I usually wouldn't tell someone until I'd gotten them invested in the relationship. Now you think I'm odd.

TED: Have you ever been to therapy?

RIGBY: Oh, yeah.

TED: I don't think you're odd.

RIGBY: You do, I can tell.

TED: No, you're kind of endearing.

RIGBY: ...in an odd way?

TED: Okay, yeah, oddly endearing.

RIGBY: Your turn. Tell me something "real" about yourself that's not in your profile.

TED: What do you wanna know?

RIGBY: Random question—what's your biggest fear?

TED: That's easy. Heights. Is that a problem?

RIGBY: Why would it be a problem?

TED: Because your profile mentions you love skydiving, and I feel like I should warn you that anything above six feet is pretty much—it's no-man's land. So if that's a deal breaker...

RIGBY: It's not a deal breaker.

TED: Good.

RIGBY: You'd love it, though. Skydiving—it's amazing.

TED: I won't.

RIGBY: You won't love it? Or you won't do it?

TED: I just can't. The height thing. It's...

RIGBY: You're afraid.

TED: Yeah. I get too freaked out. Heights, they make me vomit.

RIGBY: Have you ever done it?

TED: Done what?

RIGBY: Jumped out of a plane.

TED: No.

RIGBY: Because I'm HIV-positive.

TED: What?

RIGBY: And I won't live in fear.

TED: Wait—

RIGBY: I don't believe in being sick. I don't believe in wasting time. I don't believe in parachutes.

TED: Wait, what?

RIGBY: I have HIV. It's what I have.

TED: That just came out of your mouth. We were talking about sky-diving and that just, it just...where'd that come from? In the conversation—where'd that come from?

RIGBY: You wanted "real."

TED: Okay, but...that's how you told me? Just like that? Before we've even gotten our table? You just...said it?

RIGBY: I don't know how much more real I can get.

TED: Right, of course.

RIGBY: Might as well get it out of the way.

TED: Thank you. I think.

Beat.

So, uh...are you...healthy?

RIGBY: I'm healthy.

TED: Good, okay...

RIGBY: I think I just killed the conversation.

TED: No...I just need to think for a second.

RIGBY: Okay.

Beat.

I've never been here. Well, I've been here emotionally, but that's not what I mean. I mean this restaurant. I've never been to this restaurant.

TED: It's good. I've lived in LA for six weeks and I've already eaten here twelve times.

RIGBY: You keep track?

Ted nods.

So what do you like to eat when you come here?

TED: The salmon. It's the best thing on the menu. It's the only thing I eat here now.

RIGBY: The biggest decision you have to make tonight is what you're gonna eat.

TED: I don't need to decide anything else?

RIGBY: Not tonight. But...I want to be clear about one other thing.

TED: Okay.

RIGBY: You understood what I meant when I said I don't believe in parachutes, right?

TED: I'm not sure.

RIGBY: You know that I wasn't talking about parachutes.

TED: What do you / mean—

RIGBY: I mean: if you really want to *be* with me—I mean, if you aren't afraid—I mean, if you really want a completely unique connection—then: let's jump out of the plane together.

> *Ted suddenly realizes what Rigby's saying.*
>
> *Lights shift.*

SCENE THREE

Two months later. An office at a talent agency.

Ted sits across from Marcus.

MARCUS: You're a good actor.

TED: Thank you.

MARCUS: You are. You're talented. I'm not talking out of my ass here.

TED: I appreciate that. Thank you.

MARCUS: And you've got a great look. You've got heartthrob potential.

TED: Really? That's crazy. I never thought of myself as a heartthrob.

MARCUS: You are. You're handsome. You're gonna drive the girls wild. And you've got nice abs, I can tell. Lemme see.

Ted awkwardly lifts the bottom of his shirt. Marcus motions for him to take it all the way off. He does.

And you have the talent to back up your look, which is rare. I think you're the real deal, you've got the whole package.

TED: It's amazing to hear you say that. Thank you.

MARCUS: You're welcome, Ted.

As Ted puts his shirt back on...

TED: So that means you're gonna sign me, right? That's what you're saying?

MARCUS: Can I just say one more time how talented you are?

TED: Okay...

MARCUS: I want to encourage you to use that talent.

TED: Give me a chance to shine and I will.

MARCUS: I believe that.

TED: I've been waiting for my shot.

MARCUS: And you should get it.

Beat.

TED: So, um, Marcus...?

MARCUS: Yeah?

TED: I kinda feel like we're talking in circles here.

MARCUS: We are. Definitely. Talking in circles.

TED: You think I'm talented.

MARCUS: Very talented.

TED: And I have a good look?

MARCUS: Yes.

TED: Then are you gonna sign me or not?

MARCUS: It could happen...but I need to ask you a question.

TED: Okay.

MARCUS: I'm gonna ask you this question. I want you to think about your answer, then keep it to yourself. Don't give me an answer right away, okay? Promise you'll be straight with me.

TED: I promise.

MARCUS: And if the answer's no, I want you to promise me you won't be offended.

TED: Okay...

MARCUS: I just, I have to ask...Ted, are you gay?

Quick beat.

Now stop, don't answer, because if you *are* gay, and I *do* sign you, I don't want to know you're gay, because then when people ask me, "Is Ted Emerson gay?" I can tell them, "No," and it'll sound like the truth because as far as I know, you aren't.

Beat.

But are you?

TED: I thought you didn't want me to answer.

MARCUS: I don't. Just think. Because if I'm gonna represent you, I need to know what career I'm building. And the truth is, if you want me to make you a movie star, you can't be a gay. Gay guys don't become movie stars—not if they're out of the closet. That's just the way it works. And I get a gay vibe from you. So. If you think you might be gay and you want me to turn you into a movie star, I'd suggest you keep the gay thing a secret.

TED: Right now I'd be happy just booking a job—

MARCUS: You gotta think bigger than that, Ted. Because you're talented. You can be a character actor or a star. But I've already got enough character actors, so if that's the path you wanna take, then you can walk out that door right now. But if you want to be a star...if you want to be a star, we should keep talking. Just think about it for a second, okay?

Long beat.

Okay. Now I'm going to ask you the same question. But this time, I want you to answer.

TED: Alright.

MARCUS: Are you gay, Ted?

TED: No.

MARCUS: Then I would love to represent you.

Lights shift.

SCENE FOUR

A few hours later.

Ted, in his bedroom, a drink in one hand, a cordless phone in the other. Shirtless. He checks himself out in a mirror on the wall, looking for that "heartthrob potential" Marcus mentioned. He makes a phone call.

In another part of the stage, Sophie, 16, answers her rotary phone.

SOPHIE: Hello?
TED: Hey sis.
SOPHIE: Teddy?
TED: Yeah, it's me.
SOPHIE: Oh my god, Teddy—you called!
TED: I'm sorry. / It's good to hear your voice—
SOPHIE: It's so good to hear your voice! Yeah. I thought you would've called yesterday, though.
TED: I know. Happy belated birthday. I'm sorry I missed the real thing.
SOPHIE: It's not like it was a big one or anything...
TED: Just your sweet sixteen. I'm a *shit*, you know?

SOPHIE: Yeah.

TED: I can't believe my sister's sixteen years old.

SOPHIE: I know.

TED: It's crazy.

SOPHIE: *I know.*

TED: I miss you. I wish I was there. Was it good?

SOPHIE: It was really good. You should call more.

TED: I'll make it up to you. One of these days. I will. So / how are—

SOPHIE: So how's—

TED: Sorry.

SOPHIE: You first.

TED: No, you.

SOPHIE: I was gonna ask, how's Los Angeles?

TED: Oh.

SOPHIE: That good, huh?

TED: It's a strange place.

SOPHIE: What's strange about it?

TED: There's just a lot of fucked up people here. Sorry, I didn't mean to say / "fuck."

SOPHIE: You can say "fuck" if you want.

TED: Well, I can, but you can't—

SOPHIE: I'm sixteen now, Teddy. I can say whatever I want.

TED: I'm not so sure about that—

SOPHIE: No, it's true. I told Mom and Dad, I told them: "I'm sixteen now and I can talk however the fuck I wanna talk and you can't be fucking dictators about it."

TED: You didn't actually say that to them.

SOPHIE: I fucking did.

TED: How did they respond?

SOPHIE: Well you know I'm their favorite...

TED: They said it was okay?

SOPHIE: I think they think it's a phase. That if they let me talk however I fucking wanna talk then I'll grow out of it. But it's not a fucking phase.

TED: I can't believe they said it was okay.

SOPHIE: I know!

TED: So that's how you talk now?

SOPHIE: Pretty fucking much.

TED: That's messed up.

SOPHIE: I know. So you fucking hate LA?

TED: I just get homesick.

SOPHIE: Then fucking come home.

TED: It's not that bad.

SOPHIE: Come on—fucking come home.

TED: *Sophie.*

SOPHIE: What?

TED: You know I can't go back there, so shut up, okay?

SOPHIE: Sorry.

TED: It's okay.

SOPHIE: I wasn't thinking—So...

Beat.

...what were you gonna ask me? Before. When I interrupted you.

TED: Right, that...

SOPHIE: Yeah, that. Huh...?

TED: How are Mom and Dad?

SOPHIE: Oh.

TED: That good, huh?

SOPHIE: Actually, they're really good.

TED: Really? But Mom...is she...um...

SOPHIE: She's healthy.

TED: Yeah?

SOPHIE: Yeah, she's in remission.

TED: She is? Wow.

SOPHIE: I know.

TED: So that means they're done / with the chemo?

SOPHIE: They're done with the chemo.

Beat.

They got all of it. Supposedly, at least.

TED: Okay, good. That's great, that's really great...

SOPHIE: She looks good. And she's already feeling stronger.

TED: That's...yeah, that's great. That's...yeah, yeah...

SOPHIE: You know Mom. She's a fighter.

TED: Yeah. Okay, good. That's amazing. Good for her...yeah.

Beat.

And Dad, he's...

SOPHIE: Nothing new, really. He's just Dad.

TED: Good. Okay. Good.

SOPHIE (*changing the subject*): Have you met any movie stars yet? In Los Angeles?

TED: No, but—

SOPHIE: I was sure you'd meet a movie star by now.

TED: Not yet.

SOPHIE: When you meet one, promise you'll get me their autograph. I don't care who they are—just get their autograph. That's how you can make up for forgetting my birthday. Do we have a fucking deal?

TED: We have a fucking deal.

SOPHIE: Even if they're not very big. But try to get someone big.

TED: I'll get you someone good.

SOPHIE: Cool.

TED: Hey, Sophie—guess what? I got an agent.

SOPHIE: Really? That's so great. That's fucking exciting.

TED: I guess.

SOPHIE: No, fucking congratulations, it's fucking amazing. You're gonna make it, Teddy. You are. You're gonna fucking make it.

TED: I don't know. We'll see.

SOPHIE: I believe in you.

TED: Thanks, sis.

Beat.

Hey, do you think you could, maybe, um...

SOPHIE: What?

TED: No, never mind. I should probably get going.

SOPHIE: What were you gonna say?

TED: I'm glad you're sixteen.

SOPHIE: That's not what you were fucking gonna say.

TED: Just...do you think you could tell Mom and Dad? That I got an agent. And...that you believe in me?

SOPHIE: Sure.

TED: Yeah, if you could tell them that, I'd really appreciate it.

SOPHIE: You know, if you really wanna talk to them, you could call them yourself. They have a phone line too.

TED: Don't—

SOPHIE: It's only—and I'm sorry to be so blunt here, but—

TED: For real, just shut up—

SOPHIE: But sometimes I wanna be like, "grow some fucking balls" to you, you know?

TED: Yeah, I know...

(*trying not to crack*)

...Goddamnit.

SOPHIE: Are you okay, Teddy?

TED: Yeah.

No. I mean, yeah, but—. I just...this is awful what I'm gonna say, but...I just...

I'm just surprised to hear that she's better and...I wasn't expecting you to say that, and so...I'm a little flustered...I, um...I just...

SOPHIE: What is it? Say it.

TED: It's just that when she got sick,
there was a part of me that was...
happy, I guess...
or, not, happy, really—
that sounds so terrible—
but I was hopeful, I guess.
Hopeful that she'd—
How do I...?

Beat.

I thought that maybe the cancer would,
I don't know,
make her reach out to me.
Maybe she'd stop shutting me out.
Maybe I wouldn't be her homosexual son anymore.
Maybe I'd just be her son.
You know, without any qualifiers.
I'd just be her son. And...well...
I've been waiting for that to happen ever since the diagnosis.
I've been waiting for us to have that moment—
that moment when we both cry

and forgive each other

and tell each other how much we still love each other

even though we stopped saying it a long time ago.

And then when you said she was in remission, I just...

I know I'm supposed to be happy, but...

it kind of kills me because...

we never had that

moment of

reconciliation

that I kept hoping

the cancer

was gonna make us have.

You know?

SOPHIE: Whoa.

TED: Did I say too much?

SOPHIE: Just—fucking whoa.

TED: I said too much.

SOPHIE: No. I hate that mom makes you fucking feel that way.

TED: Don't even get me started on dad.

SOPHIE: I mean, *fuck*. You need to fucking tell her that. Not in those exact fucking words, but—

TED (*backpeddling, not wanting to go there*): Okay, I have to go now, so—

SOPHIE: Ted, I'm fucking serious—

TED: Oh, but one last thing? I love you, Sophie—I do. And I don't mean to be a dictator about it, but: I hate the way you're talking now. I really, really hate it. So if you could try to stop saying "fuck" so much, I'll try to start calling you more. Okay? Do we have a deal?

SOPHIE: Sure, yeah. We have a deal. I'll fucking try.

Lights shift.

SCENE FIVE

Four months later. Ted's bedroom.

Ted/HollywoodTed sits at his laptop, typing.

VOICE OF AOL: You are now entering the "Male4Male4Romance" chatroom.

Beat.

Ted reads through profiles.

VOICE OF AOL: FunSport9 has sent you an Instant Message. Do you accept?
HOLLYWOODTED: Yes.

FunSport9 appears. They talk as they type.

FUNSPORT9: 'Sup?
HOLLYWOODTED: Not much. You?
FUNSPORT9: Horn.
HOLLYWOODTED: Huh?
FUNSPORT9: *Horny.*

HOLLYWOODTED: Oh.

FUNSPORT9: Into?

HOLLYWOODTED: Complete sentences.

FUNSPORT9: What?

HOLLYWOODTED: You asked what I was into. I'm into complete sentences.

FUNSPORT9: LOL.

    Stats?

HOLLYWOODTED: I told you.

FUNSPORT9: You didn't tell me your stats.

HOLLYWOODTED: No, I told you I'm into complete sentences.

FUNSPORT9: What?

HOLLYWOODTED: You said "stats?" That's not a complete sentence.

FUNSPORT9: What. Are. Your. Stats?

HOLLYWOODTED: Thank you.

FUNSPORT9: So what are they?

HOLLYWOODTED: Those are complete sentences. Thank you.

FUNSPORT9: Are you going to tell me what they are or not?

HOLLYWOODTED: They're in my profile.

FUNSPORT9: Hold on.

Beat. He reads Ted's profile.

    Nice.

HOLLYWOODTED: Thanks.

FUNSPORT9: My cock is nine inches. Cut.

HOLLYWOODTED: I gathered.

FUNSPORT9: Huh? How?

HOLLYWOODTED: From your screen name.

FUNSPORT9: Oh.

HOLLYWOODTED: "FunSport9."

FUNSPORT9: Right.

They're real inches, not AOL inches.

HOLLYWOODTED: Okay.

So...what do you do for fun?

FUNSPORT9: Do you like it dirty?

HOLLYWOODTED: What do you mean? Like—

FUNSPORT9: Do you like it dirty?

HOLLYWOODTED: Are you asking if I like to talk dirty?

FUNSPORT9: No.

HOLLYWOODTED: I don't know what you're asking.

FUNSPORT9: I mean...do you like it when things get dirty?

HOLLYWOODTED: Like, during sex?

FUNSPORT9: Yeah.

HOLLYWOODTED: Like, talking dirty?

FUNSPORT9: No.

HOLLYWOODTED: Look, I don't know what you're getting at, but—

FUNSPORT9: I like it dirty.

HOLLYWOODTED: —this is the "Romance" room.

FUNSPORT9: Are you jerking off right now?

HOLLYWOODTED: No.

FUNSPORT9: I am.

HOLLYWOODTED: That's not really what I'm looking for right now.

FUNSPORT9: Shit makes me hot.

HOLLYWOODTED: You do know this is the "Romance" room?

FUNSPORT9: You want to shit on my face?

HOLLYWOODTED: What?

FUNSPORT9: Do. You. Want. To. Shit. On. My. Face?

HOLLYWOODTED: What the fuck? That's what you meant?

FUNSPORT9: What?

HOLLYWOODTED: When you asked if I liked it dirty?

FUNSPORT9: Yeah?

HOLLYWOODTED: You were talking about shit?

FUNSPORT9: Yes.

HOLLYWOODTED: I'm not into that.

FUNSPORT9: Bye.

VOICE OF AOL: FunSport9 has exited the room.

FunSport9 disappears.

TED: This is the "Romance" room. Jesus Christ.

VOICE OF AOL: LookingForTheOne has sent you an Instant Message. Do you accept?

HOLLYWOODTED: Yes.

Henry/LookingForTheOne appears. He and Ted talk as they type.

LOOKINGFORTHEONE: Henry here. What up?

HOLLYWOODTED: Not much. You?

LOOKINGFORTHEONE: Horny.

Beat.

    You still there?

HOLLYWOODTED: Yeah.

LOOKINGFORTHEONE: I thought I lost you.

HOLLYWOODTED: No.

LOOKINGFORTHEONE: Are you horny?

HOLLYWOODTED: I guess, but I'm in the "Romance" room and I'm kinda looking for some "romance."

LOOKINGFORTHEONE: Oh.

HOLLYWOODTED: Not looking for a quick fuck.

LOOKINGFORTHEONE: Sorry.

HOLLYWOODTED: It's okay.

LOOKINGFORTHEONE: I didn't realize I was in the "Romance" room.

HOLLYWOODTED: Oh.

LOOKINGFORTHEONE: I thought I was in a different room.

HOLLYWOODTED: Okay.

LOOKINGFORTHEONE: But I can do romance.

HOLLYWOODTED: I thought you were horny.

LOOKINGFORTHEONE: I am. But ultimately...

HOLLYWOODTED: Yeah?

LOOKINGFORTHEONE: You can't read the morning paper with someone's dick.

HOLLYWOODTED: That's very romantic.

LOOKINGFORTHEONE: You know what I mean. You say you want romance—

HOLLYWOODTED: I do.

LOOKINGFORTHEONE: I want it too. I want something real.

HOLLYWOODTED: How do I know you aren't just saying that to get into my pants?

LOOKINGFORTHEONE: Even though I'm horny, ultimately I'm looking for "the one." Hence my screenname. And a little romance sounds nice. So maybe I stumbled into this room for a reason—maybe I was supposed to meet you and be romantic?

Beat.

So what do you say?

VOICE OF AOL: RigbyInLA has entered the room.

Beat.

LOOKINGFORTHEONE: Hello? Did I lose you?

VOICE OF AOL: RigbyInLA has sent you an Instant Message. Do you accept?

LOOKINGFORTHEONE: Are you there?

HOLLYWOODTED (*to LookingForTheOne*): Yes.

(*then to AOL*)

Yes.

> *Rigby/RigbyInLA appears. He talks as he types.*

RIGBYINLA: Hey, Ted.

LOOKINGFORTHEONE: I thought I lost you.

HOLLYWOODTED (*to LookingForTheOne*): Sorry, I was thinking.

LOOKINGFORTHEONE: What were you thinking?

RIGBYINLA: It's been awhile.

LOOKINGFORTHEONE: You there?

RIGBYINLA: You there?

HOLLYWOODTED (*to RigbyInLA*): Yeah, I'm here.

(*to LookingForTheOne*)

I was thinking we should meet. Everything you said...I like that you used the word *hence*...you sound like a nice guy.

RIGBYINLA: I haven't heard from you.

HOLLYWOODTED (*to RigbyInLA*): You're a freak. I don't want to talk to you.

LOOKINGFORTHEONE: Let's trade pics.

RIGBYINLA: I thought we had a connection.

HOLLYWOODTED (*to RigbyInLA*): No, we didn't.

RIGBYINLA: Look, I like you. Give me another chance.

HOLLYWOODTED (*to LookingForTheOne*): I'm sorry, I can't trade pics.

RIGBYINLA: I don't date much.

HOLLYWOODTED (*to RigbyInLA*): I wonder why.

LOOKINGFORTHEONE: Why can't you trade pics?

HOLLYWOODTED (*to LookingForTheOne*): I'm an actor. I have to be discreet.

RIGBYINLA: Because I don't meet guys I like very often.

LOOKINGFORTHEONE: What have you done?

HOLLYWOODTED (*to LookingForTheOne*): Nothing yet.

RIGBYINLA: But I liked you. A lot.

LOOKINGFORTHEONE: Then why do you have to be discreet?

HOLLYWOODTED (*to LookingForTheOne*): It's a precaution. Sorry.

RIGBYINLA: So? Ted? What do you think?

LOOKINGFORTHEONE: I'm not in the business, I don't know how all that works.

HOLLYWOODTED (*to LookingForTheOne*): And I don't have one on this computer.

RIGBYINLA: Don't ignore me, Ted. Give me another chance.

That gives Ted an idea. He clicks a button.

VOICE OF AOL: You are now ignoring Instant Messages from RigbyInLA.

Rigby disappears.

HOLLYWOODTED: If you don't want to meet me without seeing my picture, I'd understand. But there's this really nice restaurant around the corner from me that I've been dying to try. La Boheme. It looks romantic. How about tomorrow night at seven?
LOOKINGFORTHEONE: Yeah. Sounds good. Let's do it.
HOLLYWOODTED: Awesome. Hater, then.
LOOKINGFORTHEONE: What?
HOLLYWOODTED: Sorry, I meant to type "later." Not "hater."
LOOKINGFORTHEONE: Ha. Talk to you "hater" then, Ted.
HOLLYWOODTED: Ha. Yeah. Talk to you "hater," Henry.

Lights shift.

SCENE SIX

The next night.

La Boheme on Santa Monica Blvd.

Ted and Henry sit across from each other, checking each other out—coy, flirtatious.

HENRY: Do you ever...no, never mind.
TED: What is it?
HENRY: It's a weird thing to say.
TED: Say it.
HENRY: Do you ever have a compulsion to do really inappropriate things? Like, just now, I wanted to lean over and kiss you, but I stopped myself because we only met five minutes ago and that would be inappropriate.
TED: You want to kiss me? Here?
HENRY: Can I?

Ted looks around to see if anyone's looking.

TED: Okay.

Henry leans in and kisses Ted.

Ted returns the kiss for a moment, then pulls away.

HENRY: That was romantic, right?

Ted looks around again to see if anyone saw the kiss. No one is staring.

TED: Yeah, it was...very romantic.
HENRY: Do you ever have weird compulsions like that?
TED: I do, yeah. Sometimes, when I'm drinking...no, never mind.
HENRY: I said mine, you have to say yours.
TED: But yours wasn't weird, it was sweet and flirtatious. Mine is genuinely strange.
HENRY: I won't judge you.
TED: Sometimes when I'm drinking—it doesn't have to be alcohol, it can be anything—this happens when I'm sober—I have a compulsion to throw my drink in people's faces. I don't know why. I just have the compulsion. I've never acted on it, but it's strong.
HENRY: That is weird. It's really weird.
TED: I told you!
HENRY: Okay, I have another one. Sometimes when I'm doing karaoke—

TED: Wait—you do karaoke?

HENRY: Yeah.

TED: Like, religiously?

HENRY: Every Tuesday night at Fubar. Is that religious?

TED: Very.

HENRY: Now I'm embarrassed.

TED: Say what you were gonna say.

HENRY: I like to sing depressing karaoke songs. Like, when everyone in the room is feeling high because someone sang something really rousing, I like to bring the room down by finding the most depressing thing I can find in the songbook. And then everyone looks at me, like, *dude, why did you sing that song*? I think it's kind of funny.

TED: That's beyond weird. I don't even know what that is.

HENRY: Oh, and sometimes when I'm driving, I have to stop myself from driving into pedestrians.

TED: Oh my god—

HENRY: I'll see someone on the side of the road and think: "If I jerked the wheel a couple of inches, my car would swerve and hit them." And then I have to hold onto the wheel really tight to make sure I don't actually do it. It's not that I *want* to hit them; it's just, I'm aware of how easy it would be and then I have to stop myself. Which makes me worse than beyond weird because who else would fantasize about hitting pedestrians?

TED: Hello? *Me.*

HENRY: Really?

TED: I think about it all the time. Especially in LA.

HENRY: Crazy.

TED: I know.

HENRY: Your turn.

TED: I tell people I'm afraid of heights, but really / I think I'm just afraid of jumping.

HENRY: You're just afraid of jumping?

TED: How did you know I was gonna say that?

HENRY: I'm the same! It's like, if I'm on a cliff or a roof or something, it's not that I want to jump, but I'm aware that jumping is a possibility—

TED: Right—you're aware it's a path you *could* take...jumping—

HENRY: But you don't jump because—

TED: Because you're not crazy.

HENRY: Wanna hear something that is crazy? I wanna kiss you again.

Ted scans the room, uncomfortable.

TED: Oh.

HENRY: You don't want to kiss me?

TED: I do, it's just...

I feel weird kissing a guy in public.

HENRY: You kissed me a minute ago.

TED: I know, but I'm not big on public displays of affection.

HENRY: We're in West Hollywood.

TED: But I've never even held hands with a guy in a public place.

HENRY: Kiss me.

Ted leans in for another kiss.

Lights shift.

SCENE SEVEN

Three weeks later, Marcus's office.

Marcus and Ted sit across from one another.

TED: So I'm dying to know what you wanted to talk about—that you couldn't say over the phone. I mean, it must be big, right? It must be—

MARCUS: Oh it's big.

TED: Does someone want me to screen test for something? But that doesn't just happen, not without an audition. So it's an audition, right? What's it for? When is it?

MARCUS: Last Tuesday night.

TED: I don't...understand.

MARCUS: I saw you. At Fubar.

TED: Wait, what? What were you doing at Fubar?

MARCUS: I saw you. Making out with some guy. Doing karaoke with him.

TED: My boyfriend.

MARCUS: Jesus, Ted, don't say that. Don't you remember what I told you when I signed you? Now what am I supposed to tell people if they ask me, "Is Ted Emerson gay"?

TED: Are they really gonna ask that?

MARCUS: I told you I don't want to represent gay clients. I told you that.

TED: Then say I'm not gay.

MARCUS: I'm not that good a liar, Ted. Besides, your tongue was down his fucking throat. How am I supposed to lie about your orientation when I've got that image seared into my head? I can't. Which is why I have to drop you, Ted.

TED: You can't do that—just because I'm gay? That's illegal. Right? It has to be illegal.

MARCUS: No, I'm dropping you because you entered into this relationship under false pretenses. When I signed you, I asked if you were gay—

TED: Right, and you said—

MARCUS: —and you said no.

TED: You *said* to say no.

MARCUS: You lied to me.

TED: *You told me to—*

MARCUS: I can't in fair conscience represent a liar.

TED: How is this happening?

MARCUS: You can go, Ted.

Beat.

Ted? I do have other things to do. So when I say "go," I'd appreciate it if you left now.

Ted gets up. Begins to go, then...

TED: Wait, but—you're gay too.

MARCUS: No, I'm not.

TED: Yeah, you are. You're gay.

MARCUS: Are you calling me retarded?

TED: You were at Fubar.

MARCUS: It's a bar.

TED: It's a *gay* bar.

MARCUS: Straight guys never go to gay bars?

TED: Were you at Fubar with your girlfriend?

MARCUS: No.

TED: Do you have a girlfriend?

MARCUS: Yes. She's magnificent.

TED: I don't believe you.

MARCUS: Believe what you want to believe.

TED: I think you're kinda gay.

MARCUS: Gay people think everyone is gay.

TED: I just think that...if you *are* gay...we should watch out for each other...we shouldn't hurt each other...Like, we shouldn't discriminate against ourselves...or live in this bullshit society where we're afraid to kiss our boyfriends in public because of assholes like you.

MARCUS: I'm sure fantasyland must be a nice place to visit, but I've got work to do, so...

TED: Right. Okay, sorry, my bad. I'll go then.

MARCUS: But wait—Ted? Before you go?

TED: Yeah?

MARCUS: Do you wanna suck my dick?

TED: *What*?

MARCUS: Do you. Want. To suck. My dick.

TED: You're joking, right?

A beat.

Then, serious:

MARCUS: Yeah.

Lights shift.

SCENE EIGHT

A week later, Ted's office.

Ted's at his desk, typing.

VOICE OF AOL: LookingForTheOne has sent you an Instant Message. Do you accept?
HOLLYWOODTED: Yes.

Henry appears, also in an office. He and Ted talk as they type.

LOOKINGFORTHEONE: Hey / babe.
HOLLYWOODTED: Hey babe.
LOOKINGFORTHEONE: Jinx, you owe me a coke.
HOLLYWOODTED: I typed it first.
LOOKINGFORTHEONE: I hit "enter" first. How's work?
HOLLYWOODTED: It's bad. It sucks. Call me.

Henry picks up his phone, dials. Ted's phone rings. He answers it.

TED: Computer Entertainment World, how can I help you?
HENRY: Hey.
TED: Hey.

HENRY: Sorry work sucks.

TED: It's boring, that's all. I spent the whole morning sending my headshot out to new agents.

HENRY: You'll get one.

TED: I don't know, we'll see. Anyway, my day just got better.

HENRY: Why?

TED: Because you called me.

HENRY: Awwwww.

TED: I can't believe I said that.

HENRY (*sweet*): You're so gay.

TED: I know.

HENRY: So corny.

TED: I know. I'm that guy. That corny, gay guy.

HENRY: Such a cheeseball.

TED: Stop it—

HENRY: You are, I love you.

Quick beat—Ted smiles—when—

It.

TED: What?

HENRY: I meant to say "it."

TED: "It" what?

HENRY: "I love it," like: I love that your day just got better because I called you. I love it—that's what I love.

TED (*enjoying the moment, egging him on*): But that's not what you said.

HENRY: I know.

TED: You said—

HENRY: It was a mistake. Oh my god I'm sorry—that came out wrong too. The "mistake" thing.

TED: It's okay.

HENRY: No, let me start over. I do love that your day got better because I called. I *love* that. And I *like* you—a lot. But I meant to say I love "it" because...Look, I'm not really ready to go there yet. It's still early for us. I mean, we haven't even [slept together yet]—well...I mean, don't get me wrong. I feel like we're almost there, I'm just not ready to say it yet. Not over the phone. You know what I mean?

TED: Sure, yeah.

HENRY: You really do? You're not upset?

TED: Well, of course—yeah. I mean, I'm not upset. I understand what you're saying. I totally agree. I like you too, so—yeah. / So, um—what do you want to do tonight?

HENRY: Good, so—what do you want to do tonight?

TED: Jinx, you owe me a coke—

HENRY: You already owe me one.

TED: We're even, then. Listen—I was thinking you could come over to my place.

HENRY (*blurting it out*): I don't want to have sex with you. I mean—I do—god, everything I'm saying is coming out wrong—I just don't want to have sex with you tonight. I like how we started out romantic, and I want to wait until it's the right moment. Can we do that? Say something.

TED: Sure, yeah. We can do that.

Ted's call waiting starts to beep.

HENRY: Really? That's okay with you?

TED: Listen, I'll be right back, okay? I'm getting another call.

HENRY: Okay.

Ted answers the other call.

TED: Computer Entertainment World, how can I help you?

In another part of the stage, Sophie appears.

SOPHIE: Teddy? Teddy?

TED: Sophie, what's wrong?

SOPHIE: Fuck, Teddy. Fuck, just—fuck.

TED: What's wrong? Something's wrong.

SOPHIE: She's fucking dead, Teddy. I can't even believe it, she's just—fucking—

TED: Wait, mom?? But she was better—

SOPHIE: She's dead, she's just fucking dead—she's—

TED: That's not true—

SOPHIE: She's just fucking dead.

TED: Stop saying that.

SOPHIE: But Teddy—

TED: That can't be true, you said it was gone—the cancer—

SOPHIE: It was gone—and then she felt this other lump—and we took her to the hospital and it was back and then she was gone—I didn't even have time to pack her overnight bags, she—she just fucking died.

TED: She couldn't have, because if she was sick you would've called me—you would have called me, right?

SOPHIE: Teddy—

TED: Why didn't you call me?

SOPHIE: Because Dad told me not to, okay? And it happened so fast. I'm, I'm sorry, Teddy.

TED: So she's...she's really...

Ted hangs up the phone. Sophie disappears.

Henry gets disconnected. He types.

LOOKINGFORTHEONE: Are you there? We got disconnected. Ted? Are you there?

Lights shift.

SCENE NINE

A week later, the Abbey.

Henry sits alone, waiting.

Ted enters, distracted.

TED: I'm sorry I'm late.

HENRY: It's okay.

TED: We should order.

HENRY: It's so good to see you...I missed talking to you this week, you haven't been online...

TED: I'm sorry. I just...

HENRY: For a couple of days, I was worried you blocked me on Instant Messenger. That's ridiculous, right?

TED: Completely. Totally.

HENRY: So is everything okay? You're not, like, distant because of the thing I said before, on the phone? You know, the love thing? Because then you cancelled our date that night and it's been hanging in the air and—

TED: I don't want to be here.

HENRY: What? Where do you want to be?

TED: About what you said on the phone...I know you don't want to say you love me yet, that it's too early, but I don't fucking care about too early anymore because I've been thinking a lot these last few days and I'm not afraid to say it: I totally fucking love you. I do. And about the sex thing, and how we haven't had it yet, I know you want to be romantic and wait, and that's awesome, but—can we go somewhere? Now? Anywhere. Will you have sex with me? Make love to me. Fuck me. All of the above. Now. Tonight. Please? Henry? Say something.

HENRY: This is messed up. I'm sorry.

TED: What's messed up?

HENRY: What I'm about to say. I should have told you this earlier...*shit.*

TED: Told me what?

HENRY: I was gonna say something in the chatroom when we first met, but I didn't. And then I was gonna say something on our first date, but I didn't. And then on the second date, and then the third, and then I said the thing about us waiting to keep it "romantic." And now, all of a sudden, here we are and I haven't told you.

TED: Could you please—

HENRY: I'm such a fuck, I'm sorry.

TED: —just—look, I don't know what you're freaking out about, but I do know we've been dating for four weeks and three days—and yes I've been counting—and we've had ten dates—and we haven't had sex yet. Which *has* been romantic. It has. And I'd like the first time to be equally romantic, but right now I need to be close to someone—no, not someone: you—I need to be close to *you*—I need to touch *you*—I need to be with *you*.

So if we could make the romance happen, like, now...I'd really appreciate it.

HENRY: I understand, I just...I need to ask...what's your status, Ted?

TED: My status?

HENRY: Your HIV status. What is it? It's, it's, it's...

TED: It's / negative.

HENRY: It's negative.

TED: Yeah.

HENRY: I thought so.

TED: And yours is...?

HENRY: Yeah, mine is...not negative. And I guess I should have told you that before I started to fall for you because then it wouldn't hurt so much if you decided you wanted to walk out that door right now. Which, if that's what you want to do, I won't hate you, you know? I'll understand. But, well...I won't lie to you, it's gonna hurt. And, so...

TED: This is so surreal.

HENRY: I'm sorry.

TED: No, it's surreal because I've been here before. I mean, I've had a similar conversation.

HENRY: And?

TED: And I can't walk out that door. Not from you.

HENRY: Shit. I was hoping you'd hurt me. Because then I wouldn't have to say the next thing I'm gonna say which is gonna hurt you: I don't want to see you anymore, Ted.

TED: What do you mean?

HENRY: I don't want to see you. I don't know how to be more clear than that.

TED: Wait—what? What are you saying?

HENRY: I got it five years ago, and before I had it, I'd never met anyone else who had it and I didn't really know it was something that you were supposed to—I mean *really supposed* to—still worry about. Because who dies of AIDS anymore? People in Africa, but not—it just wasn't on my radar. And then I found out my friend Mark had it, and Mark—he was, like, twenty-two, and...we'd been in a relationship, like, a year earlier, so...I got myself checked out, and...

Beat.

Since I found out...I haven't...you know, done anything...with anyone who wasn't positive. I did that on purpose because I never wanted to have this conversation. Then I met you, which was an accident. I didn't mean to go into the "romance" room. There's this chatroom, it's the "Poz4Poz" room...and I didn't even realize I was in the wrong room until you were like: "This is the romance room," and being romantic was nice, so I went with it. And then you happened. And...and I just...I don't know how to do this. With someone who's not...

TED (*reaching out for Henry, touching him*): They're called condoms. We can wear them. That's how you do it. We can work this out. We can be safe.

HENRY: Thank you for not freaking. That's great. But I still think we should break up.

TED: I love you.

HENRY: Don't make this harder than it / already is.

TED: No, I love you—*I love you.*

HENRY: Don't say that.

TED: Why can't we try to work this out? If you want to go to a counselor or something, we can do that—we can figure out how to make this work, how to be safe, how to—

HENRY: You're really saying all the right things, you are—

TED: I'm just saying what I feel—

HENRY: Which makes this harder, because I don't want to hurt you and—

TED: Then don't hurt me—

HENRY (*adamant*): But condoms break, Ted. They break. And if I gave this thing to you...

TED (*desperate*): No, we can figure this out—

HENRY: If we're together, I'm always gonna be worried—

TED: Don't be worried—

HENRY: —about hurting you.

TED: You're not gonna hurt me—

HENRY: So I'm just gonna leave now—

TED (*pulling Henry closer*): If you walk out that door, you're gonna hurt me—

HENRY: But I won't be killing you.

TED: Don't be crazy. Nothing's gonna happen—

HENRY: But what if it *does*, Ted? Because if something happened to you, I'd kill myself. Really. I would. And I can't go through that. Please—I love you, too—but this is over, okay?

A kiss. Ted breaks down.

Henry exits.

Lights shift.

SCENE TEN

Ted's bedroom.

Three weeks later.

Ted has a drink in one hand, his phone in the other. He's trying to keep his shit together. He makes a call.

Sophie appears and answers her phone.

SOPHIE: Hello?
TED: Happy un-birthday, sis.
SOPHIE: Teddy!
TED: Do you still celebrate your un-birthday, or are you too old for that?
SOPHIE: You're never too old for an un-birthday. I can't believe you remembered the actual day.
TED: I know, right? So, wow. Sixteen-and-a-half. You're almost seventeen.
SOPHIE: I know.
TED: Believe me, the second half of sixteen is way better than the first half.
SOPHIE: It better be.
TED: It is—it's generally underrated, the second half of sixteen.

So...you're not saying "fuck" anymore?

SOPHIE: Not too much.

TED: When you answered the phone, I was expecting you to say "fucking hello."

SOPHIE: I kinda grew out of it.

TED: That's good, that's good.

SOPHIE: I just feel like, since I'm getting older, it's time to be more sophisticated.

TED: It suits you.

SOPHIE: So how are you? I miss you. How's LA?

TED (*putting on a good act*): It's great, it's amazing.

SOPHIE: And your agent—he's sending you out?

TED: All the time, yeah—yeah.

SOPHIE: That's great. So you're getting jobs?

TED: Oh yeah, I'm working all the time. Like I said, it's great.

SOPHIE: Anything I can see?

TED: Not yet, no. But down the road. It's crazy, it's like all of my dreams are coming true.

SOPHIE: I'm so happy for you, Teddy. I'm just...I'm so glad things are working out.

TED: Thanks, Sophie. Hey, uh—

SOPHIE: Yeah?

TED: I'm still really sorry I couldn't go out there for the funeral. It's just...I've got so much going on, it's hard to get away.

SOPHIE: It's okay, I know—that's what I figured. I miss you, that's all.

TED: You too. I miss you too.

> *Ted's losing his composure more and more, but he tries not to let his sister know he's crying.*

SOPHIE: How's Henry? Are you guys still—
TED: Oh, yeah, yeah—we're great. I think he's the one.
SOPHIE: Wow.
TED: Yeah.
SOPHIE: That's so good. I can't wait to meet him one of these days.
TED: You will. You'll love him. Hey—I've been meaning to ask, like: how's dad?
SOPHIE: He's just dad.
TED: Honestly, I don't really know what that means anymore.
SOPHIE: Listen, if you really want to know how he is, you should call him.
TED: If he wanted to talk to me, he would call me.
SOPHIE: He's not gonna make the first move, Teddy—
TED: I don't want to be the only one who tries.
SOPHIE: But I think he has a lot of regrets and I think you're one of them—
TED: Thanks, that makes me feel *really* good.
SOPHIE: No, that's not what I mean. I don't think he regrets who you are—I think he regrets not knowing you anymore.
TED: Does he ever mention me?

SOPHIE: When I walk around our house, it—it's so empty and—it's impossible to not feel the absence of both mom and you. But you're not dead...And...our family is...*incomplete*. I feel it and I know he feels it too—

TED: But does he ever mention me? At all?

SOPHIE: No, Teddy—

TED: See?

SOPHIE: But he's lonely. And if you two would just talk—I know he loves you too—I just think something drastic has to happen—we need to get the two of you face to face—

TED: Change the subject? It's your un-birthday. Let's talk about you.

SOPHIE: But, Teddy—

TED: No, let's talk about you.

SOPHIE: Fine. I just finished reading *Crime and Punishment* for my AP English class.

TED: Was it any good?

SOPHIE: It was, it was really good. And I know this is gonna sound melodramatic, but when you read something like *Crime and Punishment*, it kind of puts your own problems in perspective. Because we don't have it nearly as bad as they do. I mean, Raskolnikov murdered someone. And Sonya's a prostitute. And Katerina Ivanovna is dying of consumption. And all of the other characters are going through really difficult, trying times, too, and, well, my point is that...our family? We have it easy in comparison.

TED: Are you sure we're talking about the same family?

SOPHIE: I'm being serious! And I was thinking about you and dad—and about how things were between you and mom when she passed, and—

TED: I don't want to talk about any of that—

SOPHIE: That's fine—no, it's okay—I won't talk about that. Back to the book: okay, so, at the end of the book, Raskolnikov, this murderer, he has nothing, right? He's done these really bad things, he's lived this really bad life—and he's going into exile. And you think he's lost. He's a goner. But then Raskolnikov gets down on his knees and he kisses the ground and he asks God for forgiveness, and Sonya, this prostitute...she finds it in her heart to love him, to forgive him, to believe that he can be good again. And at first, when I finished the book, I didn't really understand how she could do that. I mean, how could she love this guy who murdered an innocent woman? How could she, you know?

TED (*getting emotional, trying to keep it in*): It's just a book, Sophie—

SOPHIE: But then I decided that she did it because no one else believed in him. And that's not really very fair. I mean, everyone needs someone, right? Even the worst people—especially the worst people. We all need someone. Like, if everyone gave up on Raskolnikov, he really would be lost. Which is why the prison system is so fucked up—excuse my language, I'm trying not to say that word anymore—but it's like, we throw people away in prison and then they come out and of course they're still gonna be bad because we've told them they're bad and we've done nothing to help them—if we could rehabilitate them, instead of just punishing them, if we could give them hope, somehow, then maybe—oh my god, it's so frustrating. But my point is: if you believe in someone—if you believe they can change—if you give them love, hope...then...even the worst person can change.

Beat.

And, well, I'm just saying all of this because, Dad...I know he's been really fucking shitty to you. And I say "fucking shitty" because there's really no other more polite way to describe how he's been. But, maybe, if you forgave him...maybe he'd come around. I know he loves you, but maybe he'd finally be able to show it for once. He's lonely. *I know that.* And if one good thing could come out of Mom dying—if it could bring the two of you together—then maybe her death wouldn't be so pointless? I just think that, with Dad—he's stubborn and he's old-fashioned and it's easy to give up on him—but if you keep trying, if you show him that you believe, then he's gonna change. One of these days. He'll show you that he loves you. If you just stick in there. Do you hear me at all? I mean, I'm not even seventeen yet, but I think I'm saying some really smart things here, and you should listen to me.

TED (*stifling tears, changing the subject*): Guess what I got you for your un-birthday?

SOPHIE: Did you hear anything I said?

TED: I got you an autographed picture of Orlando Bloom.

SOPHIE: Wait, what—

TED: I know how much you like him—

SOPHIE: You're not supposed to say what a present is before someone opens it.

TED: I'm sorry—

SOPHIE: But you got me Orlando's autograph?

TED: I told you I'd score you someone big.

SOPHIE: Holy crap. Okay, I'm not done talking about the other thing, but: Oh. My. God. How did you meet Orlando Bloom?

TED: I didn't actually meet him. There's this guy I met online who happens to be working on a movie with him.

SOPHIE: You know I'm in love with Orlando.

TED: I know.

SOPHIE: You don't understand how exciting this is. I think I just peed my pants a little bit.

TED: I put it in the mail—you should get it tomorrow.

SOPHIE: I can't wait to see it!

TED: I have to go, okay? I have an audition.

SOPHIE: Oh, okay. Break a leg...

TED: I love you, Sophie.

SOPHIE: You too.

Ted hangs up, Sophie disappears.

Lights shift.

SCENE ELEVEN

The next day, Basix Café.

Ted sits at a table, alone. Waiting. Rigby approaches him.

TED: Rigby, hey.
RIGBY: Hey.
TED: Thanks for, um...for—
    Have a seat.

Beat.

    Thanks for meeting me here.
RIGBY: I'd given up on ever seeing you again in person.
TED: You're mad at me—why are you mad at me?
RIGBY: Did your sister like the autograph?
TED: She loved it, yeah.
RIGBY: Good. I'm not mad at you. I just didn't think we'd ever get a second date.
TED: The thing you said about not wearing parachutes, it was fucked up—
RIGBY: And then, out of the blue, months later, you email me asking for Orlando Bloom's autograph—
TED: You mentioned the movie in your profile.

RIGBY: And *then* you *finally* ask me on a second date. It's a little back-asswards, is all.

TED: I want to say something. I need to say something.

RIGBY: Then fucking say something.

TED: But first, there's...I'm feeling a lot of tension between us and I just: do you think we could start over? Let's pretend that we never had that first date, and I didn't take a long time to finally call you, and you're not mad at me. Could we do that?

RIGBY: Yeah, sure—okay. I could pretend.

TED: Okay, good. Good. So now we've wiped the slate clean.

RIGBY: And this is our first date then?

TED: I can pretend if you can.

RIGBY: This is a date, right?

TED: It's a date. We met online. I recognize you from your profile. Which I read ten times.

RIGBY: That's obsessive.

TED: Or thorough.

RIGBY: You look good. You look handsome.

TED: Thanks.

RIGBY: You did something to your hair. Since the night we didn't meet.

TED: I got a haircut.

RIGBY: It looks sexy.

TED: I don't know how to...
    I'll just...I was thinking...
    Listen—

(*launching in*)

I wasn't gay in high school.
There was this girl, though: Sheena.
She was gay.
She came out of the closet when we were freshmen. I don't know anyone who was friends with her, but we all knew who she was: she was "the gay girl."
That's just how we knew her.
Now, like I said,
I wasn't gay back then,
so I wasn't "the gay guy,"
I was just "*a guy*"—
...and Sheena, well...
Sheena was the only gay person I knew and she was as gay as they get.
She was, like, Super Gay, you know what I mean?
So then, flash forward to senior year, it was time to take our senior pictures and they told us we had to wear either:
a tuxedo or a gown.
And Sheena...
Sheena chose the tuxedo.
Which was the wrong choice. For girls, you know.
Because when our principal saw her photo, he, like, flipped out.
It became, like,
this huge thing.

Then, in the end, they decided not to put Sheena's picture in the yearbook.

They just didn't put it in.

So, like, if you look back at my senior yearbook,

it's almost as if Sheena didn't exist.

Okay. Then:

the summer after I graduated from high school,

before I went to college,

my dad's best friend, Jack, was staying with us.

I'd known Jack my whole life and I really looked up to him.

He was kind of, like, a second father, in a way.

Like, better than my real dad.

And Jack was going through a tough time.

He was trying to work things out with his wife—

and in the meantime, he was staying with us, until he got back on his feet.

Why am I telling you this?

Okay. Anyway.

Long story short:

Jack and I spent a lot of time together that summer.

And there was this one night when Jack and I were talking...

we had this conversation

and I remember he asked me:

"Are we friends?"

And I was like: "Yeah."

And then he was like: "Do you want to be closer friends?"

And I didn't know what he meant, and so I was like: "Yeah."
And then a couple of weeks later,
I found out what he meant.
We were alone at the house and...
I mean, he was my dad's best friend.
I looked up to him.
I trusted him.
And...
He told me he...
Well.
So, anyway,
then I went off to college—the University of Wyoming in Laramie.
Which was obviously not very far from home,
but I moved into the dorms so at least it felt like I'd moved away—
I had decided
I wasn't gonna be gay in college.
And the first day I was there,
there was this luau party,
and I met this guy Scott,
who was totally gay and totally cute,
and we hung out all night,
and I started to think, you know:
maybe I should rethink this whole "I'm-not-gonna-be-gay-in-college" thing.

But then,

that night,

I went back to my dorm room,

and, well...

We had these dry erase boards? On our doors?

You know, so people could leave us messages if we weren't home...and someone had written the word 'faggot' on my door. Which totally freaked me out, you know, so then the whole "I'm-not-gonna-be-gay-in-college" thing went back into effect.

Now, flash forward to senior year:

Not much had changed.

I was still living in the dorms.

I still wasn't gay.

And I still had a crush on Scott.

The day before graduation, a bunch of us, including Scott, went out to this field, this place we used to hang out.

We got drunk, we got high, we had fun.

And then we started playing truth or dare.

Now you have to imagine this group:

We were all in the drama department,

so all of the guys were gay

and most of the girls were straight

and then there was me.

And I was nothing.

Okay, now:

back to the field:

we're playing truth or dare...

and someone asks one of the guys,

"Who in this group do you most want to fuck?"

And the guy was like: "Ted."

And then someone else says: "We should all answer that question."

And I was next, and I didn't know what to say, so I asked if I could think about it for a few minutes—

which I'm sure was, like, the gayest thing I could have possibly said.

So they skipped me and everyone else in the group answered the question.

And all of the guys,

including Scott,

said they wanted to fuck me.

And all of the girls,

including the lesbian,

said they wanted to fuck *Scott*.

And then it was my turn to answer the question again.

And I decided, "I'm gonna tell the truth for once."

So I said I wanted to fuck Scott too,

figuring it was a semi-safe thing to say

because all the girls had said it

and maybe they'd think I just wanted to fuck his personality or something.

At least, that's what I told myself.

Anyway,

then we all drove back to campus.

Scott and I were in different cars.

And it took me awhile to get back to my dorm room because I was kind of drunk. But when I did get back,

I went into my room and I noticed:

the red light

on my phone

was blinking—

which meant I had voicemail.

It was Scott.

Now—

Scott was moving to New York the next day after graduation

and he wanted to tell me that he'd had a crush on me

ever since the first day of school

and he was wondering if I'd come over to his room and spend the night with him.

He figured he might as well ask

before he moved to New York and lost the opportunity and would I call him and give him an answer?

So I hung up the phone

and before I even had time to process what I'd just heard

the phone rang.

It was Scott.

And he was like: "Did you get my message?"

And I was like: "Yeah."

And he was like: "So, what do you think?"
And I was like: "Um, no. I'm sorry, but no."
And he was like: "Have a good life then."
And I was like: "You too."
And then he hangs up.
And then I was so mad at myself because
I wanted to sleep with him so badly
but he caught me off guard, you know?
So I sat there for a few minutes
just, like, so upset with myself,
and then I decided:
I'm gonna go over there.
I'm just gonna go over there.
And so I did.
I walked outside.
I walked to his place, which was two dorms over.
I walked inside.
I walked upstairs.
I walked to his room.
And I stood.
Outside.
His door.
I just stood there,
trying to get up the courage to knock.
But I couldn't.
I couldn't knock.

I just stood there.

I just...stood there...for twenty minutes,

I'm not even exaggerating, I'm not an exaggerator, I just stood there

getting angrier and angrier at myself.

For not knocking.

For not doing anything.

For being this pathetic loser.

I just stood there.

And then I walked back home to my dorm room.

And I never saw Scott again.

Anyway,

then I grew up.

And, like, here I am.

And where is that exactly?

Let's see:

My mom died hating me,

and my dad's still alive, but he won't talk to me.

And my agent dropped me because I'm gay even though I think he is too.

And I just want one good thing to happen in my life.

And I'm in love with this guy who could be that good thing but he has HIV and he broke up with me because he doesn't want to hurt me. And, well...

I was thinking about you,

and I was thinking about the thing you said at the end

of the date

that we didn't have,

and, um, I was thinking...

that...

we can have a connection, you know?

Because you can hurt me.

I mean,

I just want one good thing,

so...

I was hoping maybe you could help me with that.

RIGBY: What are you saying, Ted?

TED: I want you to give it to me.

Blackout.

INTERMISSION

ACT TWO

SCENE TWELVE

Six months later. Crunch Gym.

Neal runs on a treadmill. Rigby enters. He runs next to Neal. Neal checks Rigby out. Rigby checks Neal out. They race each other for a few beats. Finally, Rigby stops running, walks to Neal's treadmill, and shuts it down. Then, without ado:

RIGBY: I'm Rigby.
NEAL: I'm Neal.
RIGBY: You wanna fuck?
NEAL: I'm parked in the garage.

Lights shift.

SCENE THIRTEEN

Ten minutes later. A parking garage.

Both men are mostly clothed—they're in public—as Rigby fucks Neal up against the inside of an open car door. Rigby talks easily as he fucks. (Neal's more caught up in the sex—breathing heavily.)

RIGBY: So what do you do?
NEAL: Huh—what?
RIGBY: For a living.
NEAL: I'm discreet—
RIGBY: You won't tell me?
NEAL: Uh—uh—no—
RIGBY: We're in a parking garage...
NEAL: Oh man, yeah—
RIGBY: ...fucking...
NEAL: Right there—
RIGBY: ...and you're worried about being discreet?
NEAL: Dude, right there—
RIGBY: Alright. Don't tell me what you do.
NEAL: Man, shut up—just keep—oh god—doing what you're doing, right there—
RIGBY: Right, okay—

(*thrust*)

I was just thinking...

(*a moan*)

Oh God—

(*regaining composure*)

There's just...my head, it's...filled with all this clutter,
these things I don't want in there—
I've been thinking about that a lot.
Then there's other things, parts of your brain you wish you could
still get to—
Fuck your ass is tight.

(*lost in the sex for a few thrusts*)

Anyway, like all the shit you learned in school you didn't think
you'd ever need—
like grammar things,
like where to fucking put apostrophes—
you lose those things and you look stupid.
Because you know that crap's filed away in some drawer in your
brain that you just don't have access to anymore—

NEAL: Whatever man—harder.

RIGBY: You like that, huh?

NEAL: That's good—

RIGBY: Good. So like I was saying:
> instead of having access to those things that you fucking lost—
> those facts—you're stuck with this other shit that's right there at the surface.
> Shit you wish you didn't remember.

(*re: the sex*)

> Fuck man, fuck that feels good.

NEAL: Yeah...

RIGBY: Yeah. So anyway,
> it's like that fucking cliché—
> you know, the don't-think-of-an-elephant cliché—
> this one time, I went over to the Scientology Center,
> just to see what those guys were really up to.
> Because you hear crazy things—
> Assholes coming from outer space to get us, and shit like that.
> But who knows?
> I mean, who *really* knows unless you've checked it out?
> If you don't check it out, it's just all these—

(*a sex moan*)

oh god—

—apocryphal stories.

So I went to the Center,

the big blue building on Sunset,

and they give you all these tests, all these personality tests, or

what have you.

Just a huge fucking waste of time, really.

One of the tests—they sit you in a room—and they tell you not to

think of a pink box.

"Don't think of a pink box."

They say it, like, a dozen times.

"Don't think of a pink box."

"Don't think of a pink box."

"Don't think of a pink box."

And then they leave you in the room for ten minutes—and all

you're thinking about the entire time—

is that stupid

pink box

that you're not supposed to think about.

This was a couple of years ago and I still remember that stupid

pink box.

Anyway—oh god—*oh man*—

Anyway, I'm just trying not to...

Ohhh—

fuck—

A couple more thrusts. They pull their pants up. Neal takes off his shirt and uses it to wipe up the mess he made on the inside of Rigby's car door.

NEAL: Thanks, man.

Neal exits. Rigby is alone.

Lights shift.

SCENE FOURTEEN

A few nights later. Rigby's bedroom.

Ted sits at Rigby's desk, typing on the computer.

VOICE OF AOL: You are now entering the "Poz4Poz" chatroom.

Ted reads through profiles.

Rigby enters the bedroom, eating cereal. He leans over Ted, gives him a kiss on the neck.

RIGBY: You want me to make you breakfast?
TED: It's nine p.m.
RIGBY: I'm getting a late start. So you want me to make you something? I make a mean omelette.
VOICE OF AOL: LookingForTheOne has entered the room.

Henry appears in another part of the stage.

TED (*immediately distracted*): I'm good, thanks.

Rigby begins a workout, which continues through the scene. Starting with push-ups.

VOICE OF AOL: HollywoodTed has sent you an Instant Message. Do you accept?

HENRY: Wow. Okay...you can do this.

(*to AOL*)

Yes.

Ted and Henry talk as they type.

HOLLYWOODTED: Are you there?

LOOKINGFORTHEONE: Hey.

HOLLYWOODTED: You actually responded to my IM. How are you?

LOOKINGFORTHEONE: I'm sorry. After we broke up, I—

HOLLYWOODTED: You don't have to explain yourself.

LOOKINGFORTHEONE: No, I want to. I'm sorry I never returned your calls or your emails. And I'm sorry I blocked your screenname. It just...it hurt too much, not being able to be with you, and I had to get you out of my head. I'm sorry. I went to Arizona for a few weeks. My cousin owns this spa in Tucson. And I'm getting into meditation, and—

HOLLYWOODTED: We can talk again, though? That's why you responded to my IM?

LOOKINGFORTHEONE: Actually, I've been meaning to get in touch with you. I've been meaning to call.

HOLLYWOODTED: Yeah?

LOOKINGFORTHEONE: I was really stupid.

HOLLYWOODTED: What do you mean?

LOOKINGFORTHEONE: I was there in Arizona, meditating, chanting like an insane person, and all I could think of was you. I'm sorry about that night at the Abbey. I was an idiot. We can figure this out.

HOLLYWOODTED: Oh my god, wow.

LOOKINGFORTHEONE: We can be safe. I've been doing the research. It's not as difficult as I thought. I was so afraid of hurting you, but we can make this work. If you'll still have me. Are you there?

HOLLYWOODTED: Of course I'll still have you. Are you kidding? And you wouldn't hurt me anymore. You can't.

LOOKINGFORTHEONE: What do you mean?

HOLLYWOODTED: Can I call you?

LOOKINGFORTHEONE: Sure.

Ted picks up his phone and dials.

Henry's phone rings.

Rigby finishes his push-ups, starts chin-ups.

Henry answers the phone.

HENRY: Hey.

TED: Hey.

HENRY: What's going on? What's up?

TED: It's so good to hear your voice.

HENRY: You too.

TED: Yeah.

HENRY: Really good.

TED: I got tested. I'm positive.

HENRY: Wait—what?

TED: I'm positive.

HENRY: What do you mean?

TED: I didn't get it from you. I got it *for* you.

HENRY: *What?*

TED: So you wouldn't have to worry about hurting me.

HENRY: Wait—what?

TED: Because I love you.

HENRY: Are you fucking insane?

TED: I love you. I've never felt this way before.

HENRY: You're joking, right?

TED: I'm completely serious.

HENRY: *You got it for me?*

TED: I told you—I love you.

HENRY: That's...that's...that's the sickest thing I've ever heard / in my life.

TED: No—I mean—I can understand how you might see it that way, but—I love you.

HENRY: I don't even know what to say to you.

TED: Say that you love me too.

HENRY: Oh my god, I don't even know how... / Ted, how could you—

TED: You love me. That's why you left me. Because you loved me too much. You didn't want to hurt me. Now you don't have to worry about that anymore. I hurt myself so you don't have to, so now—

HENRY: Stop talking.

TED: —we can be together.

HENRY: Just stop talking. Stop talking.

TED: You were afraid of me getting it. Now you don't have to be.

HENRY: No, listen to me. I'm healthy right now. I'm doing well. Which means I'm nauseous and I'm tired and I've had really bad diarrhea for the last month. It's my medication. It isn't fun. It's not something I'd choose to go through. Now don't get me wrong—if I have to choose between this or death, I'll choose this. But for you to *choose* to go through this. I can't even imagine. How could you do this? We were supposed to work this out, we were going to work this out, this isn't how this conversation was supposed to go. How could you possibly think this would make me want to be with you?

TED: You don't understand.

HENRY: No, I don't.

TED: I miss you. I feel so alone. Please—

HENRY: I hate that you did what you did. I hate that.

TED: But I love you.

Henry hangs up. Dial tone.

Henry?

Henry sits at his desk, in shock.

Ted hangs up his phone.

RIGBY: You okay?

TED: I'm gonna go for a walk.

RIGBY: That was Henry? On the phone?

TED: I can't talk about it right now. I need some air.

RIGBY: You want me to come with you?

TED: No.

Ted exits.

Rigby sits at the computer, starts typing.

VOICE OF AOL: Goodbye HollywoodTed.

Sound of a door closing. Sound of a door opening.

VOICE OF AOL: Hello RigbyInLA. You are now entering the "Poz4Poz" chatroom.

Henry's still on-stage, but he's moved away from his computer. An IM ding draws him back to the computer screen.

VOICE OF AOL: RigbyInLA has sent you an Instant Message. Do you accept?
HENRY: Sure.

He types in his response.

Yes.

Rigby and Henry talk as they type.

RIGBYINLA: Hey.
LOOKINGFORTHEONE: Hey.
RIGBYINLA: Horny. Wanna hook up?

Beat.

Sigh. Henry's not in the mood for this.

LOOKINGFORTHEONE: You know what? ...Maybe this isn't a good idea.

RIGBYINLA: What do you mean?

LOOKINGFORTHEONE: I mean, read my profile.

RIGBYINLA: I did. You sound hot.

LOOKINGFORTHEONE: Then read my screenname.

RIGBYINLA: "Looking For the One."

LOOKINGFORTHEONE: Exactly. I'm not looking for "a" one, I'm looking for "the" one. I'm looking for an LTR. So even though I can respect that you're horny and wanna hook up, we're not a match.

RIGBYINLA: I can do a Long Term Relationship.

LOOKINGFORTHEONE: You're not just looking for a quick fuck?

RIGBYINLA: I'll take one if I find one. But I'm looking for something more substantial.

LOOKINGFORTHEONE: Then could you tell me something about yourself that proves you're not full of shit? Sorry to be blunt, but guys on AOL are full of shit and I don't know what to believe.

RIGBYINLA: You can be anyone you want to be on the internet—

LOOKINGFORTHEONE: Exactly.

RIGBYINLA: But for me, I feel like the internet is the only place where I can truly be one-hundred-percent myself. Here we are—I don't know what you look like; you don't know what I look like. All we have is our words. And I could sit here and type lies to you, I could tell you anything I wanted to, I could tell you I'm a doctor, I could tell you I'm British, I could tell you I've got a fourteen-inch dick. Whatever. But if we ever meet, the truth is gonna come out—you're gonna find out I'm not a doctor, you're gonna realize my British accent is for shit, and you're gonna see that my dick's only twelve inches.

LOOKINGFORTHEONE: Ha.

RIGBYINLA: But look at the alternative: I could tell you the truth about me. I could tell you I'm a gaffer, I could tell you I was born and raised in Encino, and I could tell you my dick is about eight inches. And if you don't like gaffers from Encino with eight inch dicks, well, it's your loss. Who cares? We can stop talking right now, you don't ever have to talk to me again, and I haven't lost anything—but I think you do want to talk to me. I just sent you my number. Call me.

Henry dials. Rigby answers his phone.

RIGBY: Hey.

HENRY: Hey.

RIGBY: So to finish my thought, if you choose to be totally honest and upfront with me too? Well, then, we might be onto something. So the benefits of lying on the internet, really, are zero—and the potential for gain if you tell the truth—it could be huge. And your screen name, LookingForTheOne. Well, I am too. I know the internet seems like a weird place to find him, but I'm running out of places to look in the real world. Besides, we're already talking about who we are, who we *really* are—and that's what I'm looking for. I mean, a hook-up? Sure, if I can find it. Hook-ups are fun. But sex is easy. If I can find someone who's willing to have a real, honest conversation, then...That's what I want. This—this is what I want. I want "the one." Are you ready for that?

HENRY: Yes.

RIGBY: So, do you want to meet?

HENRY: Tuesday's karaoke night at Fubar.

RIGBY: Sounds fun.

HENRY: You know, I just realized I haven't even seen your picture. How am I gonna know what you look like tomorrow night?

RIGBY: After that whole speech? About connections and how it doesn't even matter that we don't know what the other one of us looks like?

HENRY: Well, yeah.

RIGBY: There's a picture in my profile.

HENRY: I haven't even read your profile.

A beat, as Henry reads.

Wait—I've read your profile. I mean, before today.

RIGBY: Have we met?

HENRY: No, but I've seen you. In other chatrooms.

RIGBY: I don't recognize your screenname.

HENRY: In the "romance" room.

RIGBY: I've been there.

HENRY: You're in the "Poz4Poz" room. Aren't you positive?

RIGBY: Yes.

HENRY: So what were you doing in the "romance" room?

RIGBY: I can't go into the "romance" room if I'm positive?

HENRY: That's not what I'm saying.

RIGBY: It better not be.

HENRY: Your profile says you only bareback.

RIGBY: I told you—I'm always completely honest when I'm online. If that's something you don't like—we're still in our living rooms. We didn't risk anything. We can forget each other.

HENRY: But you're positive.

RIGBY: So?

HENRY: SO USE A FUCKING CONDOM.

RIGBY: Whoa—

HENRY: Do you *really* only bareback?

RIGBY: That's what my profile says.

HENRY: Why?

RIGBY: I like natural sex. I like to feel actual sensation when I fuck, not fucking rubber. And I'm totally open about that in my profile, so people know what they're getting into, and if they don't like it, they don't have to talk to me.

HENRY: What's wrong with you?

RIGBY: There's nothing fucking wrong with me. I like sex.

HENRY: But you're positive.

RIGBY: I am acutely aware of that, yes. Thank you for reminding me.

HENRY: So why don't you say that in your profile, if you're so fucking honest?

RIGBY: People should assume.

HENRY: But they don't assume. It's your responsibility to tell them.

RIGBY: I do tell them if they ask. Besides, we're in the fucking Poz4Poz room, so chances are—

HENRY: But they could get it.

RIGBY: I don't have to worry about that. If I'm with someone who isn't worried about getting it, then why should I care? I'm healthy—I'm still fucking healthy. I'm fine.

HENRY: You're not fine.

RIGBY: I've lived with the disease for years. And I'm not gonna worry anymore. Let someone else worry for a change.

HENRY: That's murder, you lying hypocrite asshole.

RIGBY: Then I guess we should both be happy we're not at Fubar because we obviously aren't meant for each other.

(*pointed*)

Hater, dude.

Henry disappears.

Lights shift.

SCENE FIFTEEN

An hour later. Sunset Boulevard.

Ted stands on a freeway overpass— looking down at the 101 below. The sound of cars and traffic. Ted looks awful, unkempt. He is unhinged. Rigby enters.

RIGBY: Didn't you hear me honking?

TED: What are you doing here?

RIGBY: You called me. I couldn't find a place to park.

TED: What do you mean?

RIGBY: I kept driving by. I couldn't pull over. You didn't hear me honking?

TED: No.

RIGBY: I parked on Western.

TED: I forgot you were coming.

RIGBY: What did Henry say to you?

TED: He loves me, and he hates me—but I don't want to talk about him. I took Sophie's advice. I called my dad. I made the first move. I reached out. And he—he doesn't want me. He doesn't wanna know me. He said he—oh god, he—. And now—now—there's no hope there, there's no hope. So—so—so what do, what do I have?

RIGBY: You have me.

TED: No, I don't—

    I don't have anyone—

    I have this disease.

    And I don't want you.

    Jesus, I can't even talk to my sister anymore. I can't tell her what I've done—

    we used to tell each other everything, but some things—

    some things are...impossible to tell a person.

    Oh my god, just—what have I done?

    Why did you give it me?

    Why did you do it?

RIGBY: Because you asked me for it.

TED: But why did you say yes?

RIGBY: I like you.

TED: What's that supposed to mean?

RIGBY: I thought we could have a connection. And now we do.

TED: That's all? That's why you...

RIGBY: I'm not gonna let other people tell me what I can and can't do.

    You wanted it, so I gave it to you.

TED: Okay, but...I don't...I don't want it anymore. Take it back.

RIGBY: I can't.

TED: You can have it. I don't want it.

RIGBY: It doesn't work that way.

TED: You can't take it back?

RIGBY: No.

Ted crumples into Rigby's arms, then to the ground. Really beginning to lose it.

TED: Why won't my dad take me back? Why won't he answer my calls? Sophie said he was gonna change. And I just—I hate it out here. I fucking hate it. I wanna go home.

RIGBY: Let's go back to your place.

TED: That's not what I mean—no.

RIGBY: I'll make you a bowl of soup or something.

TED: I'm not afraid of heights anymore—

Ted steps over the ledge. Suddenly he's gone. No warning. The sound of cars screeching below. Panic, alarm. Rigby's heart races.

Lights shift.

SCENE SIXTEEN

A week later. Basix Cafe in West Hollywood.

Rigby stands outside, waiting.

Steve enters.

RIGBY: Hey.

STEVE: I'm SoccerStud69.

RIGBY: I figured.

STEVE: You look better in real life.

RIGBY: Thanks.

STEVE: Nothing against your photos. It's just—you never really can tell online—the last guy I met, his photos must have been twenty years old.

RIGBY: You look better than your photos too.

STEVE: You think?

RIGBY: Well I can't completely tell. Most of the photos you sent weren't of your face.

STEVE: Look, I'm not really hungry for dinner. I live around the corner. You wanna...?

RIGBY: Yeah, I "wanna."

Lights shift.

SCENE SEVENTEEN

Steve's apartment. About ten minutes later.

Steve and Rigby enter, already making out.

STEVE: Do you party?
RIGBY: I try not to.
STEVE: Mind if I do?
RIGBY: It's cool.
STEVE: Hold on.

Steve exits.

RIGBY: Nice place!
STEVE: What?
RIGBY: You have a nice apartment.
STEVE: Thanks!
RIGBY: I'm so fucking horny right now.
STEVE: What did you say?
RIGBY: Where did you get this couch?!
STEVE: Ikea!
RIGBY: I wanna fuck your brains out on it!

Steve re-enters with a pipe.

STEVE: Yeah?
RIGBY: Yeah.
STEVE: Awesome.

Steve lights the pipe, takes a hit.

You sure you don't want any?
RIGBY: I try not to.
STEVE: It's your funeral.
RIGBY: Give me a hit.
STEVE: Cool.

Rigby takes a hit. Steve takes another hit.

Fuck, man.
STEVE: Yeah.
RIGBY: Feels fuckin' good.

Rigby takes another hit. Steve peels off Rigby's shirt, starts kissing his stomach.

RIGBY: That feels fucking good, too.
STEVE (*looking up at Rigby*): I'm Steve, by the way. I don't think I ever said—

RIGBY (*uninterested*): Hi, Steve.

He pushes Steve's head back down.

They continue to grope at each other.

STEVE: Fuck, you're hot.
RIGBY: Listen, I should probably tell you—

Steve isn't listening.

STEVE: Fuck me. Now.

He paws at Rigby, kissing him.

RIGBY: I need to tell you I'm—
STEVE: You're fuckin' hot man.
RIGBY: —positive.
STEVE: Yeah, I'm certain: you're hot.
RIGBY: That's not what I meant. I said I'm positive.
STEVE: Stop talking, dude.
RIGBY: Not a question, a statement.
STEVE: Fuck me.
RIGBY: I just thought—
STEVE: You listening to me?
RIGBY: You should know—

STEVE: I said stop talking already.

RIGBY: —what you're getting yourself into.

STEVE: Just stop talking and get your dick in me, okay?

They kiss.

Lights shift.

SCENE EIGHTEEN

The next morning.

Rigby and Steve are sprawled out on the ground, naked. Steve, who is awake, shoves Rigby, who is asleep.

STEVE: Wake up.

He shoves Rigby again.

    Wake up.
RIGBY (*groggy*): Hey.

Steve makes a romantic gesture. He runs his hand through Rigby's hair. Or he kisses him. Or he bites his nipple.

STEVE: What's your name again?
RIGBY: I don't think I ever told you.
STEVE: I'm Steve.
RIGBY: I'm Rigby.
STEVE: Did we have fun last night?
RIGBY: You don't remember?
STEVE: I was pretty fucked up.

RIGBY: That shit'll kill you, you know—crystal.

STEVE: You did it too.

RIGBY: I try not to, though. You shouldn't do it.

STEVE: I can take care of myself, thanks.

RIGBY: Sorry, I just—never mind.

STEVE: What?

RIGBY (*genuine*): It's just—you seem like a really nice guy, I'd hate to see you screw up your life.

STEVE: Really?

RIGBY: Yeah.

STEVE (*touched*): Thanks.

Beat.

Hey, could I ask you something?

RIGBY: Sure.

STEVE: And since we don't really know each other, you can be totally blunt and honest. Just feel free to tell me the truth, okay?

RIGBY: Okay.

STEVE: Was I any good?

RIGBY: In bed?

STEVE: Yeah.

RIGBY: We went at it all night.

STEVE: Is that a yes?

RIGBY: Yes.

STEVE: You're not just being nice?

RIGBY: *We went at it all night.*

Yeah—you were good.

STEVE: Okay. Cool. Good to know.

RIGBY: No problem.

STEVE: Most people assume they're good in bed when they aren't—and everyone says that hot guys are really bad in bed because we don't have to try as hard—so I've always assumed I'm really bad in bed, but I've never known for sure. I never asked anyone, point blank, like I did just now. Of course, you could be lying. But whatever: I don't remember it anyway, so I'll believe you and assume I was good last night. Better to feel good about something you don't remember than regret it, right? Whatever—anyway—wait.

RIGBY: What?

STEVE: Were we safe?

RIGBY: Safe?

STEVE: You know—

RIGBY: No.

STEVE: I meant...did we use condoms?

RIGBY: I know what you meant.

STEVE: Well, did we?

RIGBY: I don't think so.

Beat.

I mean, no.

STEVE: Oh. Okay. But you're... [negative] ...?
RIGBY: We talked about this.
STEVE: Okay. I just don't remember.

> *Steve waits a moment for Rigby to answer the question, but he doesn't.*

Well, speaking of coffee—do you want me to make you breakfast, or do you need to leave?
RIGBY: You could make breakfast.
STEVE: I could make eggs, waffles—

(*noticing something on Rigby's arm*)

What's that?
RIGBY: What's what?
STEVE: Your arm. What's on your arm?

> *Rigby notices, for the first time, that there is a large, dark red stain on his arm.*

RIGBY: What the fuck?
STEVE: What is that?
RIGBY: Am I bleeding?
STEVE: Let me see.

He searches Rigby for an open wound.

You're fine.

RIGBY: I'm not bleeding?

STEVE: You're not bleeding.

RIGBY: Are you fucking sure?

STEVE: You're not bleeding. What about me? Is there any on me?

They search Steve's body for blood.

RIGBY: There's nothing on you. What the fuck is this? What the fuck's on my arm?

STEVE: It's not blood.

RIGBY: Are you sure? Are you fucking sure? I'm not bleeding anywhere?

STEVE: Calm down, you're not.

RIGBY: Then what the fuck is this?

He grabs Rigby's arm, leaning in:

STEVE: Smells like wood.

RIGBY: Wood?

STEVE: Yeah.

RIGBY: What the fuck do you mean 'my arm smells like wood'?

He licks Rigby's arm, tasting it.

STEVE: It's lacquer.

RIGBY: What do you mean?

STEVE: From the wood floor. It's lacquer.

RIGBY: What the fuck?

STEVE: Something in your sweat—you must have soaked it up.

RIGBY: I thought it was blood.

STEVE: Me too.

RIGBY: I thought it was my blood. Fuck. Jesus. Fuck.

STEVE: Are you all right?

RIGBY: Shit, fuck, yeah—I'm fine.

STEVE: You're not acting fine.

RIGBY: I'm just...seeing my blood, it—it just—

STEVE: It wasn't blood.

RIGBY: Seeing it *on me*...that was...*fuck*.

STEVE: You're fine, dude.

RIGBY: I know.

STEVE: It was just the lacquer from the wood.

RIGBY: Yeah—yeah, I know. Fuck.

STEVE: You're still not acting fine.

RIGBY: I'm great.

STEVE: Okay, then: breakfast. I could make you eggs, or—

RIGBY: I don't like my blood.

STEVE: Okay.

RIGBY: That's all—I don't like it.

STEVE: I don't really like the sight of blood either.

RIGBY: No, not blood in general, I can handle other people's blood.

STEVE: Okay.

RIGBY: I just don't like mine.

STEVE: Well, you're fine, so—

RIGBY: That's why I reacted the way I did.

STEVE: Okay. It's okay, I get it, but you're fine. Why don't I make us some eggs?

RIGBY: Yeah, um, *no*.

STEVE: What do you mean, *no*?

RIGBY: I'm not gonna stay for breakfast.

STEVE: Why not?

RIGBY: I just...I want to go home.

STEVE: Okay, well—

RIGBY: I need to go home.

STEVE: If you wanna do this again sometime—

RIGBY: Whatever, sure, yeah—

STEVE: You know where I live.

RIGBY: Right, listen—about last night...we didn't use condoms.

STEVE: Right, you said.

RIGBY: And I *am* positive, so—

STEVE: What?

RIGBY: Look, I tried to tell you last night, but I guess you don't remember. And it sounds like something you're worried about, so you might want to check it out.

STEVE (*trying to contain his anger*): You need to leave.

RIGBY: Don't worry, though, because if you get it, it's no worse than diabetes.

STEVE: Leave.

RIGBY: I just didn't—

STEVE: You can go.

RIGBY: —want to sleep alone—

STEVE: Please go. Please.

Rigby exits.

Lights shift.

SCENE NINETEEN

Later that night. Fubar.

In one part of the stage, Henry performs a karaoke version of a really sad song. [Perhaps "Angel From Montgomery."] Rigby listens for a beat, then exits into:

The Fubar bathroom. One toilet, no stall. Rigby sits on the toilet with his head in his hands. The door suddenly opens and Marcus enters.

[Note: Rigby and Marcus have to yell to be heard over the sound of the karaoke.]

MARCUS: Oh, sorry—the door wasn't locked.

Marcus starts to exit.

RIGBY: I'm done. I mean, I'm not using it. So you can, if you want.
MARCUS: Cool, man.

Marcus waits for Rigby to rise from the toilet and leave, but Rigby doesn't move.

So, um...

RIGBY: Right, yeah.

He stands.

Look—this is gonna sound weird, but...I can't go out there.

MARCUS: What do you mean?

RIGBY: I came in here to get away from that—the karaoke, the singing, the people. I just...needed some space, some quiet, something. I can't go back out there, that's what I'm trying to say.

MARCUS: You want me to leave?

RIGBY: It doesn't matter. I don't care.

MARCUS: Well—I really gotta piss, so I'm just gonna go.

RIGBY: No problem. I'll just...

Rigby backs away from the toilet as far as he can, but it's a small bathroom.

...stay over here.

Marcus crosses to the toilet to pee. Rigby averts his eyes.

Beat.

Marcus tries to pee, but he can't.

MARCUS: Sorry.

RIGBY: What?

MARCUS: Performance anxiety.

RIGBY: I'm not even paying attention. Pretend I'm not here.

MARCUS: Done.

    I'm not gay, you know.

RIGBY: What?

MARCUS: If you were wondering.

    I don't think I'm gonna pee. It's not working.

RIGBY: Do you want me to turn on the faucet or something?

    Hello?

(*noticing*)

    Are you jerking off?

MARCUS: Come on—join me.

RIGBY: I thought you weren't gay.

MARCUS: I'm not.

RIGBY: Then what are you?

MARCUS: I'm discreet.

RIGBY: Look, man—put your dick away, okay?

MARCUS: Sorry—I didn't mean to offend you—

RIGBY: Kiss me.

MARCUS: What?

RIGBY: Please. Kiss me.

MARCUS: I don't do that.

RIGBY: You don't kiss?

MARCUS: Are you messed up or something?

RIGBY: I just need to touch someone. Not sex, but—

MARCUS: I think you're kind of fruity.

RIGBY: I need to be close to someone. Closer than sex.

MARCUS: You know, I don't usually go for the faggy shit, but you're actually kind of hot. Let's go back to my place and fuck.

RIGBY: You won't kiss me? You won't hold me?

MARCUS: I told you—I'm not gay. Let's fuck.

RIGBY: Okay, sure—fine—whatever. But you'll hold me afterwards—

MARCUS: Maybe, man—if that's what you need—

RIGBY: I just need to be close to someone. Anyone. But I should tell you something.

MARCUS: Yeah?

RIGBY: I've seen a lot of messed up shit. And I've done a lot of fucked up things. I haven't slept in seven days. It's just—it isn't worth it anymore—any of it.

MARCUS: Look, I don't need your baggage—

RIGBY: Just listen to me—

MARCUS: Do you wanna fuck or not?

RIGBY: I'm a man, you know? Not some faggot.

MARCUS: Whatever you say. We can be men together. Let's go fuck.

RIGBY: Okay, good—yeah. That sounds really good. Just one other thing—

MARCUS: Did you hear me? I don't need your baggage. Let's go.

RIGBY: But do you have any condoms? Because I don't usually use 'em—but I'm fucking HIV positive, and—

MARCUS: Wait, whoa—you're poz? Sorry dude—not a match.

RIGBY: You don't wanna fuck?

MARCUS: Not anymore, man. Sorry.

RIGBY: That's okay, we don't have to fuck. If you wanna jerk off, you can go back to doing that. Just don't go back out there. I lost my friend. And I need to connect with someone. Could you please be that someone for me tonight?

MARCUS: That's not gonna happen, dude—sorry.

RIGBY: Could you please hug me?

MARCUS: Get away from me. I don't even know you.

RIGBY: Two minutes ago when you didn't know I was poz, you wanted to fuck and now you won't even hug me?

MARCUS: I don't know you. I don't wanna hug some guy I don't know.

RIGBY: I don't have the fucking plague. Touch me. Fucking touch my hands, hold my hands—

MARCUS: I'm gonna go.

RIGBY (*stopping him*): But we can be totally safe. I just need a real, human connection. Not with my dick. Something real. I'm looking for the one, you know?
Not "a" one, "the" one.

MARCUS: I know I'm the one who came on to you in the first place, and you almost seem like a nice guy, but this isn't happening. Look, I get a lot of pussy—but between you and me, sometimes I like dick. I'm not gay, it's just what I like. But since none of my friends and business associates know that about me, I have to be super discreet about the dick I sample. I can't go around getting HIV. I just can't do that. And I know you're thinking, but if we're safe, then we're cool. But that's not cool to me. I have a rule: I don't cross the status line. I just don't do it. It's like, I have some clients who work in film, and they ask me why I don't ever get them TV work, which they want because they know there's a lot of money in it, which is true and not true at the same time, but the reason I don't get these film clients of mine TV work is that I know that if they cross over into TV, they're never gonna be known as film actors again. People say that's changing, but I don't believe it's true. They see Meryl Streep doing a movie on HBO and they think they can do a movie on HBO, but she's Meryl Streep and none of my clients are Meryl-fucking-Streep. If I let them do TV, they'll be tainted and you can't get rid of that. Do you see what I'm saying? TV's just like HIV, you can't get rid of it, and you might try to say to me that some shows are safe, but fuck that. TV's still TV. And so I put my foot down. Do you see what I'm saying?
RIGBY: No.
MARCUS: Maybe I'm an asshole for saying this, but if all the poz people would only have sex with other poz people and all the neg

people would only have sex with other neg people, then eventually the disease would die away. But me? I don't wanna die.

RIGBY: Right, of course.

MARCUS: So I'm sorry, but...

RIGBY: I don't want to die either.

MARCUS: Okay, well—good luck with that.

Marcus exits.

Lights shift.

SCENE TWENTY

The sidewalk outside of Fubar.

Later that night, a little after 2 a.m.

Rigby leans against the building. Henry exits the bar, begins to walk off.

RIGBY (*calling off to Henry*): You're good.

HENRY: What?

RIGBY: Your singing.

HENRY: Oh.

RIGBY: You're still standing there?

HENRY: Yeah.

RIGBY: I'm drunk—are you drunk?

HENRY: No.

RIGBY: You were probably going home, I stopped you—

HENRY: It's okay.

RIGBY: I never give compliments to strangers. I was just thinking that I should be nice to strange people more often. Not that you're strange, that's not what I meant. But you're a stranger. That's a strange word: stranger.

HENRY: Yeah.

RIGBY: Watching you sing makes me feel like I almost know you. To be honest, you kept singing sad songs and there was a point when

I had to stop listening. You made me feel sick with it. But I felt it. You made me feel it.

HENRY: I was feeling it too. That's why.

RIGBY: I could tell.

HENRY: You're RigbyInLA.

RIGBY: Do I know you?

HENRY: The picture in your profile. I recognized you.

RIGBY: I don't. Did we fuck—you and me?

HENRY: No.

RIGBY: Did I give it to you?

HENRY: I told you, we never fucked.

RIGBY: You should really walk away. Leave me alone. Or you could hold me. Whatever. I'm a man, you know? Shit—fuck—I'm the strange one.

HENRY: You're not driving home, are you?

RIGBY: This is LA.

HENRY: What's that supposed to mean?

RIGBY: It means, how else am I supposed to get there? Of course I'm driving.

HENRY: I don't think you're okay to drive.

RIGBY: I won't get in an accident.

HENRY: Yeah, no—I don't like the idea of you driving.

RIGBY: Look, I know how I'm gonna die, and that's not how it's gonna happen.

HENRY: It's not a life sentence, dude.

RIGBY: I'm just being realistic.

HENRY: Listen, where do you live?

RIGBY: I'm a lying hypocrite. You should know that. I don't want you to come home with me.

HENRY: I don't plan on going inside. Where do you live?

RIGBY: I know I just said you could hold me, but now I'm dizzy and it might make me throw up.

HENRY: I'm taking you to your house. Tell me where you live.

RIGBY (*pointing*): That way. Off La Cienega.

HENRY: I'm parked around the corner. Come on.

RIGBY: Why are you being so nice to me?

HENRY: I should be nice to strange people more often, too. So let's go.

Henry helps him.

Lights shift.

SCENE TWENTY-ONE

A few weeks later.

Basix Cafe in West Hollywood.

Rigby stands outside, waiting. He's disheveled, like he hasn't slept in days.

Sophie enters with a map. She approaches Rigby.

SOPHIE: Excuse me, do you know where—

RIGBY: Yeah?

SOPHIE: I'm turned around. I'm looking for Sunset. Is it north or south or—

RIGBY: It's two blocks north. You're not far.

SOPHIE: Thank you.

Excuse me, are you...?

RIGBY: What?

SOPHIE: Are you...okay?

RIGBY: Why would you ask me that?

SOPHIE: You look...not okay.

RIGBY: I'm fine.

SOPHIE: Are you waiting for someone?

RIGBY: Uh...yeah.

SOPHIE: Who?

RIGBY: A guy.

Anyway, Sunset's that way, so...

SOPHIE: I'm prying—I'm sorry, I do that—I'm not from here and I guess people don't really talk to strangers in Los Angeles, but where I'm from if you don't know someone's name, you usually at least know their face, so you can pretty much talk to anyone because you pretty much already know them. In so much as anyone can really "know" a person. You know?

RIGBY: Where are you from?

SOPHIE: Just a small town.

RIGBY: Okay...so, uh...what's on Sunset? That you're trying to find?

SOPHIE: Actually, I'm looking for one of those Star Maps guys. I have my brother's car. I was gonna drive around and look for famous people's houses. But I need a map first.

RIGBY: Well—

SOPHIE: Oh my god, that sounds so stupid, but it's—true, mostly—

RIGBY: Okay—

SOPHIE: I'm just here and I...I don't know what else to do.

RIGBY: They're not really very accurate. The Star Maps.

SOPHIE: They aren't?

RIGBY: I don't think so.

SOPHIE: But you don't really know.

RIGBY: Well, I work in the business, and—

SOPHIE: What do you do?

RIGBY: I'm a gaffer.

SOPHIE: What's a gaffer?

RIGBY: I'm basically an electrician for movies.

SOPHIE: Crazy, wow. Have you ever worked with Orlando Bloom?

RIGBY: Actually, I just did his last movie, yeah.

SOPHIE: Of course...so you're the one who got the autograph.

RIGBY: What?

SOPHIE: I'm sorry. Fuck, I can't do this. I can't pretend. Orlando's autograph. That was you.

RIGBY: Pretend what?

SOPHIE: That I don't know who you are. Listen, you're waiting for a guy named Dustin, screenname: Dusty6283. Right?

RIGBY: Right.

How do you...?

SOPHIE: I made him up. I saw you online, on Ted's "friends list," and I wanted to talk to someone who knows Ted—knew Ted. So I made up that screen name, I'm Dustin. I mean, not really—my real name's—

RIGBY: Sophie. Ted's sister.

SOPHIE: Yeah. God, I just needed to get out of his place, you know? I can't sit in there and cry anymore. I've been crying all week. I had to fucking get outside. Just, fucking...I mean, anyway: do you know Teddy well?

RIGBY: I was a friend of his, yeah.

SOPHIE: I mean, you knew him?

RIGBY: Yeah.

SOPHIE: You were his friend?

RIGBY: That's what I just said.

SOPHIE: I came out here to get his stuff. We weren't really talking very much at the end. He wasn't ever the type of person who called a lot, but he was calling even less. I wanted to come out here, I was planning a surprise trip. I just miss him, you know? Sorry—*missed* him. And I want to see him. Sorry—*wanted* to see him. I thought I'd come out here and make him ditch work and we could do all the dumb touristy things he hasn't had time to do. *Didn't* have time to do. Sorry—it's really hard for me to get used to only using the past tense with him. The past tense feels very foreign. I'm not used to it yet. Do you speak any foreign languages?

RIGBY: No.

SOPHIE: I'm taking French at school and I'm really bad at it. Like, really bad. There are so many tenses, it's hard for me to keep track of all of them. Present, and past, and future, and then you have simple past, and compound past, and conditional past, and—. That's all I can think of right now. I know there are more. But I get them mixed up. Like, I'll say things like, "Tomorrow I went to the store to buy next week's baguette." Which isn't even something one would say in real life, but it's the kind of thing we're always saying in French class. And the tenses are just so hard for me to keep straight that I decided if I ever go to France, I'm gonna throw caution to the wind and use whatever tense I can remember at the moment. But, like, with Teddy, I think it's probably best for me to get the tense thing right. It's just hard.

RIGBY: So, right now, um...You're going on the Star Maps tour?

SOPHIE: I have to get out of his apartment. Like I said, it's claustrophobic.

RIGBY: I have an idea.

SOPHIE: What is it?

RIGBY: Most of the people on the Star Maps tour are either dead or they've moved and, well...why don't I drive you around? I could show you where some famous people live.

SOPHIE: You know where famous people live?

RIGBY: A couple.

SOPHIE: Why would you want to drive me around?

RIGBY: I don't have anything else to do. I was supposed to be on a date right now, remember? But that kind of got canceled.

SOPHIE: Right.

RIGBY: So, what do you say?

SOPHIE: What kind of name is Rigby, anyway? Is that, like, made up? Or were your parents just really into The Beatles?

RIGBY: My real name's Dave. There was this guy who used to call me Rigby and it just kind of stuck.

SOPHIE: The Beatles are pretty great. You can't go wrong stealing a name from one of their songs.

RIGBY: It's just...Dave sucks. There's lots of Daves in the world. I always felt more like a Rigby.

SOPHIE: I get it. I'm down with the "individual" thing.

RIGBY: Right.

SOPHIE: So, um...how do you know my brother?

RIGBY: We met online.

SOPHIE: Did you date?

RIGBY: A little bit. A couple of times. Yeah. Then we tried to be friends.

SOPHIE: Did you love him?

Beat.

Look, can I tell you something?

RIGBY: Sure.

SOPHIE: I've been in my brother's apartment for the last three days, I've been going through his things, and...
I used to think we told each other everything—that's what we always said, at least—but I logged into his computer when I got to his place and it turns out he saved all his IM conversations, and there were some things I found out,
some things he never told me,
and...

RIGBY: You shouldn't have done that.

SOPHIE: I know. So, um, anyway. It's not like I just saw you on his "friends list" or anything. I know what you guys did. And there's just...there's a lot that I'm trying to wrap my head around and...the things that I read about, about what you gave him...are those things...are they true?

RIGBY: Yeah, they're...they are. They're true.

SOPHIE: Okay, so, um...so—can I ask you something?

RIGBY: Yes.

SOPHIE: Do you know why he would do that? Why he would want that? I mean, do you know?

RIGBY: I didn't want him to die.

SOPHIE: That's not what I asked you.

RIGBY: I wanted to be with him. You have to know that—I didn't want him to die.

SOPHIE: Will you answer my question? Please? Why would he want it?

RIGBY: I don't know.

SOPHIE: That's not fair. That's not an answer.

RIGBY: He was lonely, I think.

SOPHIE: That doesn't make any sense.

RIGBY: Can I ask you something? I'm really healthy. I am, I am. They have good medication, and I'm doing well. But things were touch and go for a while there and I've never really been able to accept that this is what's gonna get me in the end—this thing that I have. It fucking sucks, you know? Because in the end, it's gonna kill me. Sure, my odds of living longer are better now, now that we have the medication, and it's good medication, I mean I'm healthy, like I said, but I'm still gonna die sooner than I should, sooner than I'm supposed to, sooner than I want to—and so, for a while, I wanted everyone else to go with me. I did—I really did. It's the only thing I wanted. And when I met your brother...

Beat. This is fucking hard.

It's nothing personal, it's just that you don't know what it's like to have the blood that I have inside me, I don't fucking want the blood I have inside of me, and if I have to die because of the blood I have inside of me, then…I should take some people with me, you know? That's what I thought. It's not nice, or kind, but we're all human, right? I'm trying to be honest, and tell you the truth. And I'm sorry, I'm sorry—I should have said that earlier—I'm sorry. It's just that—I'm telling you this because, because, because your brother was a really good person, and, you know, we kind of became friends these past few months, I mean, he didn't really have anyone, and I didn't have anyone, and we, we, we became friends, and by the time I got to know him, got to know him better, I didn't want to take him with me, that's what I'm trying to say—I mean, I didn't want him to die, I didn't, I didn't. And then when he did, when he—he did die—I mean, I know I didn't kill him, but I feel like I might as well have—and, and, and, and I know that it can't possibly even begin to compare to what you must be going through, but now that he's gone, I miss him so much, oh my God I do, I don't have too many friends, and your brother—he was a really good guy. I don't think he loved me or anything, and I probably didn't love him, or not enough at least, I didn't do it like he deserved, but we still had a couple of good dates, and I think that, in a parallel universe, or if we were different people, or if we met under different circumstances, you know, if something had been different, I really do think that, maybe, just maybe, we could have had a thing together, a real thing, a future, something, anything, because your brother, like I said, he was a really good guy, you know that, but I want you to know that other people saw it, I saw it, I knew it, he was easy to fall in love with, and no one deserves what he went through—or what any of us go through, even—but what I'm trying to say is that things shouldn't have happened the way they did, they shouldn't have. And I know that now. And I'm sorry. I'm sorry. For what I did. And I will never—I promise you—I will never. Ever. Do it again. I won't. I promise. I really do promise. So...

I don't know what else to say.

But, that's what I wanted to tell you.

SOPHIE: You said you...

RIGBY: What?

SOPHIE: You wanted to ask me something. That's what you said. You asked if you could ask me something. What did you want to ask me?

RIGBY: Just, if you could...

I mean, not right now, but...

I was wondering if maybe, one of these days, do you think you could ever...

um, for what I did, do you think...

Do you think you could ever forgive me for that?

Beat.

SOPHIE: No.

Rigby falls to his knees and cries.

Sophie kisses him on the head, then exits.

Blackout.

INTERMISSION

ACT THREE

SCENE TWENTY-TWO

2019.

A studio apartment. Nothing fancy. But it feels like a life has been lived within these walls. There are several pieces of art. A few framed photos. An overflowing bookcase.

Dave, formerly Rigby, has his back to us. He's naked. Sitting up in the bed, on his knees. He's got some gray in his hair, but otherwise he's in better shape than last time we saw him. He masturbates aggressively, as...

DAVE: That's good. Oh, yeah. That's—no, wait.

And that's when we realize there's another man in bed with him. This is ETHAN, 28. He's lying on his back, so all we can see is the top of his head shoved in between Dave's thighs.

Could you *really* suck them? Not just lick, *suck*.

That's better. That's better. Yeah. Oh, fuck, yeah, *suck my balls*.

There we go...

There we go...

Therewego, therewego, therewego.

No, no.

I had it, but I lost it.

> *Ethan drops his head back, revealing his face.*

ETHAN: You want me to suck both of them or just one of them?
DAVE: Do what you're doing.
ETHAN: But it's not working.
DAVE: That's not you, that's me. I don't always...
ETHAN: Then what should I do?
DAVE: I don't think it's gonna happen.
ETHAN: Really?
DAVE: Yeah, not tonight.
ETHAN: Don't give up.
DAVE: It's okay, I still had fun.
ETHAN: I'm not gonna let you *not* come.
DAVE: Then suck both of them.
ETHAN: So you do like both. That's all you had to say.
DAVE: Ethan?
ETHAN: Yeah?

DAVE: Fucking suck my balls as hard as you fucking can.

Ethan gets back to work.

ETHAN (*muffled*): Is that better?
DAVE: Yeah. Fuck yeah. Yeah.
    Yeah.
    Yeah.
    Yeah.
    YEAH.
    Yeah. Oh, yeah. There. There. There. THERE. Okay, there we—yeah, yeah, THERE.
    There we—
    There we—
    There we—no. That's not—
ETHAN (*muffled*): Harder?
DAVE: Yes, fucking suck them harder, Goddamnit. If you feel like you're gonna suck them off my body, it still isn't hard enough.
    OH FUCK.
    That's better.
    Okay. YES.
    Yes.
    Yes.
    Oh fuck.
    Yes.
    YES.

Fucking yes.

That's—

Yes.

Oh.

OH.

(*several moans*)

Okay, good work.

Here.

> *He hands Ethan a t-shirt from the ground. Ethan wipes himself off, then notices—*

ETHAN: This is my shirt.

DAVE: So?

ETHAN: It's covered in semen now.

DAVE: That's what happens when you use a shirt to clean yourself off.

ETHAN: Right, but—

DAVE: It gets covered in semen.

ETHAN: Yes, *but* I didn't realize it was my shirt you threw at me. I can't wear this home now.

> *Dave climbs back into bed with him.*

Neither one of them gets dressed, or bothers with covering themselves up, for the rest of the scene. They're comfortable in their nakedness together.

DAVE: Don't go home then.

ETHAN: Really?

RIGBY: Yeah. Stay the night.

ETHAN: You think we're there?

DAVE: You don't? How many times have we hooked-up? Six? Seven?

ETHAN: What's my middle name? What do I do for a living? Where did I grow up? And who's my favorite author?

DAVE: I don't know. I don't know. Just outside Chicago. And I don't know.

ETHAN: See?

DAVE: What does that prove?

ETHAN: That we barely know each other.

DAVE: Thirty seconds ago you were sucking my testicles.

ETHAN: That's a different kind of knowing.

DAVE: Then tell me those things you think I'm supposed to know about you.

ETHAN: Staying the night's a big step for me.

DAVE: I get that.

ETHAN: I like to get to know someone first. Really know someone. Before—

DAVE: That's what I'm trying to do, right now. Tell me those things.

ETHAN: Middle name, James. I'm a dancer, at least I wanted to be. I auditioned for the Joffrey and didn't get in, so I moved to LA. I've done a few music videos? But I also work at Trader Joe's, and I don't know which one's the real answer now: "dancer" or "Trader Joe's crew." I grew up outside of Chicago, like you said, hence the Joffrey thing—specifically Forest Park. And I'm gonna say Christopher Isherwood, but I'm fickle with authors. A few months ago, I would have said John Irving. But his newer stuff sucks.

DAVE: Look at that.

We're getting to know each other.

ETHAN: Your turn.

DAVE: Same questions?

ETHAN: Yeah.

DAVE: I don't have a middle name. I'm a gaffer. Born and raised in Los Angeles, with a few detours, until I made my way back here. And I don't have a favorite author.

ETHAN: Wait, hold on—

DAVE: I know the middle name thing is weird. My parents never gave me one.

ETHAN: No, I'm on the author thing. Who doesn't have a favorite author? Do you not read?

DAVE: I read a lot of books.

ETHAN: Then how can you not have a favorite author?

DAVE: I just don't.

ETHAN: What's the last book you read?

DAVE: This book called *Shark Research*.

ETHAN: *Shark Research*? This was a novel?

DAVE: You didn't say *novel*.

ETHAN: So this was a nonfiction book about researching sharks?

DAVE: And marine biology, and oceanography, and looking into their various habitats, and—

ETHAN: I understand why you don't have a favorite author.

DAVE: Looping back around to the main issue here: do you realize how many guys I've stayed-the-night-over-with who I didn't know any of these things about?

ETHAN: See—I don't do that. Sex is one thing. We all have needs. But sleeping over? I don't do that if it doesn't mean something.

DAVE: Neither do I.

ETHAN: You just said you've stayed the night over with you-don't-know-how-many guys.

DAVE: I don't do that anymore. I'm all about substance now.

ETHAN: Are you serious? What kind?

DAVE: What kind of *what*?

ETHAN: Like, meth? Or—

DAVE: *Substance*, singular. Quality.

ETHAN: Oh, I get it—sorry, I heard *substances*—

DAVE: No.

ETHAN: —and I thought—

DAVE: I get the confusion.

ETHAN: But to be very clear, you don't do *any* drugs?

DAVE: Not anymore.

ETHAN: None?

DAVE: None.

ETHAN: Good.

DAVE: You?

ETHAN: Also not anymore...

When you used to do it, did you do a lot of it?

DAVE: We all did.

ETHAN: Lots of people still do.

DAVE: Right, and I'm not lots of people. I'm Dave.

ETHAN: Dave no-middle-name, the gaffer from Los Angeles, who doesn't have a favorite author.

DAVE: I'm not into "favorites," in general. It's reductive.

ETHAN: How so?

DAVE: You aren't actually engaging with a book, or movie, or piece of art, if all you can say is it's your favorite. What are you even saying? *Favorite*. What's that even mean?

ETHAN: It means you like something.

DAVE: But don't you realize how boring that is? *Favorite*. Go deeper than that! *Anything* can be someone's favorite *whatever*. All the word *favorite* tells me is you like things. *Toddlers* like things. Don't be a toddler. Be an adult. Don't tell me something is your "favorite," tell me how it makes you *feel*.

ETHAN: Good.

DAVE: Good *what*?

ETHAN: Isherwood's books make me feel good.

DAVE: That's not an answer.

ETHAN: It *is*, technically, / an answer—

DAVE: But I'm talking about how we form relationships with the art we consume. So, let's say, for example, with Isherwood, your so-called *favorite* author. What's good about him? How does he speak to you?

ETHAN: You know how pretentious you sound right now, right?

DAVE: I do.

ETHAN: Just making sure.

DAVE: I've earned my pretentiousness. Answer the question.

ETHAN: Have you read *A Single Man*?

DAVE: Yes.

ETHAN: So I guess "good" isn't the right way to describe what that book—how it affects me. Good isn't...

Here, let me put it this way:

A Single Man isn't the kind of book I should identify with. It's about this older guy—

DAVE: Middle-aged.

ETHAN: This middle-aged guy—

DAVE: *My* age.

ETHAN: —named George, who's grieving the loss of his longterm partner—

DAVE: I hate that word.

ETHAN: Partner?

DAVE: It sounds like a business arrangement.

ETHAN: So he's mourning the loss of his *boyfriend*. And the way Isherwood writes about this emptiness George feels. It's not something I've ever gone through, personally. I mean, I've had boyfriends, but no one's ever died on me, you know? I'm not at that place in my life yet. I mean, I still have all my grandparents, even. So like—

DAVE: Jesus Christ, you're a baby.

ETHAN: —losing a partner, or a lover, or a boyfriend, or whatever you want to call him. That's not part of my lived experience yet. Not even remotely, you know?

DAVE: Not yet.

ETHAN: Right. Exactly. But Isherwood *made me* understand how it felt to go from being part of something—being an "us," one part of a whole—and then go back to being single again. But not single because of a breakup, that's a different kind of single—he made me understand the kind of single that you don't have control over, and how devastating that can be. I don't know how else to say it. I feel like you're judging me right now—

DAVE: I'm not—

ETHAN: —like I don't sound smart enough or whatever, because I used the word *favorite*.

DAVE: I promise I'm not judging you.

ETHAN: Have you ever lost anyone? Like that—like in the book?

DAVE: A few people, yeah.

ETHAN: A few?

DAVE: Life is long.

ETHAN: I mean, hopefully.

DAVE: Yeah...

Beat.

ETHAN: Did you feel that?

DAVE: Feel what?

ETHAN: Some moments end with a period. That was an ellipsis.

DAVE: I'm fine with that.

ETHAN: So you're not gonna tell me what you're thinking right now?

DAVE: No.

ETHAN: Because I *see you* thinking something.

DAVE: I'm not thinking anything.

ETHAN: That's not true, but *okay*.

DAVE: I'm not trying to make this awkward. But some thoughts...

ETHAN: There it is again!

DAVE: What?

ETHAN: Another ellipsis.

DAVE: Some things just don't need to be said.

ETHAN: It's fine, no pressure. Just pointing it out. By the way, your penis just shriveled up. That's how uncomfortable I made you.

DAVE: You didn't make me uncomfortable.

ETHAN: Look at your penis! Look at that. It didn't want to think about heavy things. It's like when you adopt a dog from the shelter and it hears a door slam and then it cowers, like—

He demonstrates with his head.

DAVE: That's the least sexy thing you could say about my penis.

ETHAN: I think your penis can handle it.

Beat.

When was the last time you cried?

DAVE: Why?

ETHAN: I saw my neighbor crying yesterday. I was coming home from work, I pulled into my space. I look over, she's in her car, crying. I was gonna ask if she needed help, but I didn't want to intrude on this private moment she was having.

DAVE: You didn't go talk to her?

ETHAN: No. But then I was trying to think of the last time I cried, and I couldn't remember.

DAVE: I used to do that, you know. Cry in my car.

ETHAN: Are you making fun of my neighbor?

DAVE: No, I'm serious. I used to cry all the time. It would just happen. It wouldn't even necessarily mean I was sad or happy. I'd just cry. I think I did it in the car so often because this is Los Angeles. We're always in our cars. It's where we get stuck with our thoughts.

ETHAN: But not anymore?

DAVE: I'm still stuck with my thoughts in my car.

ETHAN: But you said "used to." You don't cry all the time anymore?

DAVE: Honestly, I don't even remember the last time I cried. At some point the well dried up.

ETHAN: Same, I guess.

DAVE: You're too young for a dry well.

ETHAN: Are you saying there's something wrong with me?

DAVE: There's something wrong with all of us. How fucked up would it be if we were all perfect, you know? Better to just acknowledge we're all broken and stop worrying about it.

ETHAN: My mom has this framed inspirational quote in her bathroom—

DAVE: I hate those.

ETHAN: Right? I think she got it at Ikea. It says: "When they made you, they broke the mold." When I was a kid, I'd stare at those words while I was pooping and I'd think: they didn't break the mold, they broke *me*.

DAVE: Fuck.

That's—oh, man, I'm sorry you used to stare at that dumb quote and think that.

ETHAN: It's okay.

DAVE: But it's a terrible thing for a kid to think.

ETHAN: You just said "we're all broken."

DAVE: Sure, but we aren't supposed to have that realization until we're older. When we're kids...

ETHAN: The irony is, it's a nice sentiment, you know? Like, my mom was trying to say: I see you, you're an individual, be different, be yourself. But instead of feeling free, I felt pressure to be unique.

DAVE: Ikea ruined everything queer about this country. We used to have mesh thongs and hanky codes. Now we have matching bookcases and inspirational bathmats.

ETHAN: By the way, how old are you?

DAVE: Older than you think.

ETHAN: It's just...your Scruff profile doesn't list an age, so.

DAVE: I'm old enough, and you're old enough.

ETHAN: You really won't say?

DAVE: Stay the night and I'll tell you in the morning.

ETHAN: If I stay the night, I'm hungry.

DAVE: I'll make you something. Look at that, it's a perk of staying the night.

ETHAN: Can you make me a grilled cheese sandwich?

DAVE: I can do that.

> *Dave goes to the kitchen area. Gets to work.*

ETHAN (*singing*): "One morning sis won't go to dance class."

DAVE: What's that?

ETHAN: You weren't quoting *A Chorus Line*?

DAVE: I don't think so—

ETHAN: *I can do that.* That wasn't—

DAVE: No.

ETHAN (*singing*): "I grabbed her shoes and tights and all..."

DAVE: I don't know it.

ETHAN: Oh, COME ON.

DAVE (*sigh, okay, then*): "I stuff her shoes with extra socks. Run seven blocks. In nothin' flat. Hell, I can do that. I can do that."

ETHAN: I knew you were a theater fag!

DAVE: Can you do the tap routine?

ETHAN: Of course I can do the tap routine. Can *you* do the tap routine?

DAVE: *I* can do the tap routine.

ETHAN: Show me.

DAVE: I don't have tap shoes.

ETHAN: Who needs tap shoes?

DAVE: Tap dancers need tap shoes. Tap shoes are the whole point.

ETHAN: I'll do it with you. No shoes. See what you got.

DAVE: Alright.

ETHAN: Yeah?

DAVE: You can do that?

ETHAN (*singing*): "I can do that."

> *They stand together on the linoleum tile in the "kitchen" area of the apartment.*

We need some music.

DAVE: Here.

> *Dave grabs his cell. Does a quick search. The song from* A Chorus Line *plays—or something equally peppy—through a speaker on the kitchen counter. It's a tight space, but they make do, as—*

ETHAN: Can you do that?

DAVE: I can do that.

> *They tap dance. A simple routine, that shows off some skill. One of them does a move, then the other mimics him, and so on. Ethan is clearly a trained dancer. Dave, not so much.*
>
> *The more they dance, the more they enjoy themselves. Until, Ethan notices—*

ETHAN: Smoke.

DAVE: Oh, fuck.

> *Dave rushes to the stove to save the grilled cheese sandwiches. The music continues to play for a few beats as Ethan watches Dave deal with the food. Dave turns off the music. Hands a plate to Ethan.*

It's burnt.

ETHAN: I don't mind.

DAVE: You can sit in the bed.

They sit in the bed together and eat.

ETHAN: I seriously never would have pegged you for a theater fag.

DAVE: I didn't used to be. But then I worked on this movie with Alan Cumming—

ETHAN: Nice name drop.

DAVE: It's not a name drop if you work together. He was just a co-worker.

ETHAN: Sure.

DAVE: But we kinda became friends, a little bit. And when he did the revival of *Cabaret* on Broadway a few years ago, he got me house seats and...I got hooked. I sat in that dark theater with all those strangers, watching these amazing performers and I remember thinking: why have I wasted so much of my life not seeing more of this? I actually saw *A Chorus Line* last year, at New York City Center.

ETHAN: You go to New York a lot?

DAVE: I told you, I got hooked! I try to go out a few times a year and see as much as I can.

ETHAN: Do you see the look on my face right now? This is a look of jealousy.

DAVE: So they did this revival of *A Chorus Line*, one weekend only. And it was—

ETHAN: AMAZING, right?

DAVE: One hundred percent. It was phenomenal. Ridiculous. I wish I could see it again. And—okay, you want a *real* name drop?

ETHAN: Yes.

DAVE: I was sitting behind Sarah Jessica Parker.

ETHAN: You're fucking with me.

DAVE: I am not fucking with you.

ETHAN: Her show made me realize I was gay.

DAVE: So here's my Sarah Jessica Parker story from *A Chorus Line*. The show was full of all these amazing Broadway dancers, people who were in other shows, but they took the week off from their regular gigs to do *A Chorus Line*—it was the best of the best. And there was this feeling in the room, like: most of the people there were also performers, or theater people. What I'm saying is: we knew we were watching something special, right?

ETHAN: This sounds so cool.

DAVE: Just wait. So—Sarah Jessica Parker. She's a theater person too. That's how she got her start. And she's probably worked with the people on that stage. These are her people, right? And after every song, when she clapped, she put her arms up in the air, like this—

He demonstrates a high clap, hands in the air.

ETHAN: In, like, an obnoxious way?

DAVE: No—like, when you're watching the world series and the bases are loaded and someone hits a home run and you jump out of your seat because you can't contain your excitement.

ETHAN: I don't do sports.

DAVE: But you know what I mean. That kind of enthusiasm. Watching Sarah Jessica Parker watch *A Chorus Line* was like watching someone watch their favorite team win the World Series. This is a dumb story—

ETHAN: No, I like it—

DAVE: I just thought it was sweet. Seeing her be such a fan. It made her seem normal.

ETHAN: I like that.

DAVE: Do you know who Taylor Mac is?

ETHAN: Of course. Oh my God, are you friends with Taylor Mac?

DAVE: No, but I think I sucked Taylor Mac's dick once.

ETHAN: *Now* you're fucking with me.

DAVE: It was the '80s. Everyone sucked everyone's dick in the '80s. This was when I lived in New York. I only lived there for a beat. I used to go to The Mineshaft all the time—

ETHAN: I never heard of it.

DAVE: It closed before you were even born.

ETHAN: Because of...

DAVE: Yeah.

ETHAN: Fuck.

DAVE: It's a different city now.

ETHAN: Wait, you said you *think* you sucked Taylor Mac's dick. How can you not know for sure?

DAVE: It was a dark club. I know Taylor Mac went there. It's a logical conclusion.

ETHAN: Did you see a *24-Decade History of Popular Music* at the Ace? I saw the first four hours. It fucking blew my mind.

DAVE: I saw the whole thing.

ETHAN: If you're about to say you saw the / 24-hour marathon version at St. Ann's...

DAVE: *I saw the 24-hour marathon version at St. Ann's.*

ETHAN: SHUT THE FUCK UP! Do you know how jealous I am right now?

DAVE: It was as good as everyone says.

ETHAN: You're, like, one of six hundred people.

DAVE: There was this one song, in the early 1900's section, where judy asks everyone in the audience to pretend they're living in Jewish tenement buildings in Brooklyn. We were instructed to find someone nearby

and pretend they're our spouse,

and pretend we're living with aunts

and uncles

and cousins

and children,

and the place is so cramped, with so many people,

that we never have any privacy.

And Taylor Mac says:

"While I sing this next song,

I want you to breath in each other's ears

and pretend you're having sex

while everyone else is sleeping.

You have to be really quiet so you don't wake anyone up."
Something like that.
So me and this guy,
this sweet little twink who happened to be standing near me,
we hold each other while Taylor sings
and we breathe together.
There's some moaning.
A few nearly-silent gasps.
And then the song ends, and we lose each other in the crowd.
I never saw him again, but I think about him sometimes.
My Jewish tenement husband from Taylor Mac's *24-Decade History of Popular Music*.

ETHAN: That's so fucking hot.

DAVE: You wanna do it?

ETHAN: Pretend I'm your Jewish tenement husband and breathe in your ear?

DAVE: Yes.

ETHAN: I do wanna do that.

> *They lean into each other. Pressing their lips to each other's ears. And breathe.*
>
> *This goes on longer than you expect it to.*
>
> *At one point, Dave whispers something to Ethan. Something we don't hear.*

And then:

DAVE: There was a period of time. This was the late '80s. After I found out I was positive. When I was so afraid. I watched so many of my friends die. Men I'd been with. These amazing, incredible men. One day they were here.
Then...
And I knew I was next. I had it too. All I could do was wait. I pulled away from people I loved, people who weren't positive, who didn't have this fucking thing, because: what if I gave it to them, too? You hear stories about homophobic doctors afraid to touch us, who thought they could get it just from being in the same room as faggots like us—but I had sympathy for them, too. Because what if they were right? What if I breathed on you wrong and I gave it to you? We didn't know how the fuck any of it worked. We didn't know how it got transmitted. Not at first. So I pulled away from everyone. And I mean: *everyone*. I didn't want to kill people. I didn't want to be responsible for that. I pulled away. Kept to myself. Didn't even talk to neighbors. What we just did? Breathing together? Something as simple as that felt like a death sentence to me. Because I didn't know how it worked. I was consumed by fear. And then...I lived. And I continued living. Do you know how fucking mad that made me? Why, out of all the men I knew and loved who got this thing, why did I make it through? There were better men than me. I was angry, reckless. I lived in that anger a long time.

ETHAN: How did you...

    I mean, I've been on PrEP since, it feels like forever now. So I never really had to—worry about, you know. So I just—how did you—get through that anger, I guess? Is what I'm trying to...

    I don't know.

    I don't want to say the wrong thing.

DAVE: Maybe I got old. Somewhere along the line, the guilt of being here shifted into gratitude. I still don't know why I'm here. But I might as well make the most out of what I have left.

ETHAN: Have you ever been to therapy?

Dave laughs.

DAVE: Oh, yeah. Yes. A lot of it. Copious amounts.

ETHAN: That's good.

DAVE: Did I freak you out?

ETHAN: No. You're being real.

DAVE: You know...

    No, never mind.

ETHAN: Say it.

DAVE: You remind me of someone I used to know. Someone I used to be with.

ETHAN: Is that a good thing?

DAVE: It's complicated.

    I was a different person back then. This was in my angry-reckless period. It ended badly.

ETHAN: Are you still in touch with him?

DAVE: No.

ETHAN: Do you want to be?

DAVE: It's not exactly possible. But there were things that...

We ended on an ellipsis, like you said.

Or maybe it was an exclamation point? Let's just say it was a lot of punctuation.

ETHAN: Then...what if...

DAVE: What?

ETHAN: What if you pretend I'm him? Like the Jewish tenements thing. Pretend you're with him right now. Say whatever you wish you could say to him.

DAVE: I don't think that's a good idea.

ETHAN: Why not? Why not try?

DAVE: Okay.

ETHAN: So what's my name?

DAVE: You're Ted.

ETHAN: Is there anything I need to know about Ted? I have done some acting, you know. Is there anything I should imbue into the character?

DAVE: Just be yourself.

ETHAN: Okay.

Hey Dave. How's it going?

DAVE: I didn't go by Dave back then.

ETHAN: Oh.

DAVE: I went by Rigby.

ETHAN: Like the Beatles song? That's a cool fucking name.

DAVE: It was fine. I'm more of a Dave. But back then...

ETHAN: See that's a detail I needed to know. Is there anything else I should—

DAVE: No. Just—start again?

ETHAN: Whenever you're ready.

DAVE: Okay.

    Hey, Ted.

ETHAN: Rigby. Hey. How are you? / It's been—

DAVE: It's been a long time.

ETHAN: Yeah. It's so crazy seeing you like this.

DAVE: How are you, Ted?

ETHAN: I asked you first. And you didn't give me an answer, so...

DAVE: I'm okay, I guess. I'm good? Mostly. Yeah, good. You?

ETHAN: I finally got out of LA. I went back home, to...

DAVE: Wyoming?

ETHAN: That's right.

DAVE (*breaking out of the fantasy for a beat*): Really?

ETHAN (*still in it*): I mean, LA's such a shitty city, you know?

DAVE: I like LA.

ETHAN: You *would*.

DAVE: You just met the wrong people. Henry. That asshole agent— what was his name?

ETHAN: I don't remember.

DAVE: And me. We didn't make it a home for you. The city kind of ate you alive, you know?

ETHAN: Yeah...All those auditions, and dumb day jobs, and nothing to show for it at the end of the day. It's not the kind of life I wanted.

DAVE: So you moved back home? That's good. I like that. You're close to Sophie, then? I mean, obviously the two of you are close emotionally. But I mean, physically? You live near each other now?

ETHAN: Sophie?

DAVE: Your sister.

ETHAN: Yeah. She's five minutes away. We do Wednesday game nights. Settlers of Catan, mostly. Me, and Sophie, and her husband—and my guy, if I'm with someone. Sophie knows it's serious when I invite him to game night. There's been several someones, but no one who's stuck with me for the long haul, yet. It's okay, though. I'm comfortable with myself. I wouldn't have said that years ago, but it's true now.

DAVE: And...your dad? I know things were...difficult there.

ETHAN: We've been working things out. I mean, it took awhile, but he finally came around. We probably go over to his place for dinner about once a month. But we never invite him to game nights because he's terrible at Catan. He's always trying to get the Longest Road and I'm like, "Dad, stop building a road to nowhere," but he isn't a strategic thinker. It's fine. It's nice having him back in my life. Sophie and I make fun of him. We feel like a normal family, which—I mean, I don't ever remember feeling that. I never knew what that was like.

DAVE: I met her, you know. Did she tell you that?

ETHAN: Sophie?

DAVE: Yeah. She came out here once. And we met.

ETHAN: She never told me.

DAVE: She was really tough with me.

ETHAN: Because you deserved it.

DAVE: I did.

> She never told you about this?

ETHAN: She didn't.

DAVE: Probably for the best.

ETHAN: Hey, I should go? I'm here for a work thing and I've got this meeting I need to get to—

> But is there something...

> Something specific you want to say to me? Before I go.

DAVE: Just...I want to say I'm sorry.

ETHAN: Okay. Thank you, Rigby.

DAVE: I think about that night a lot. When you told me those stories from your childhood. The thing that sticks with me, for some reason—was those kids in your dorm writing "faggot" on your door. I wish I knew you then. I could have protected you, told you it was okay to be a faggot. I wish we could've been faggots together. I wish I could have shielded you from that pain. And then later—when we were together. I know I caused you more pain. And so, I just—oh God, I just—

ETHAN (*dropping the role-play*): It's okay, Dave.

DAVE: No, I need to say this. I want to ask...if things turned out differently back then, if I hadn't been who I was...do you think... Could you ever have loved someone like me?

Beat.

ETHAN: Dave?
Look at me.
I could love you, Dave. I really think I could.

Long beat.

Blackout.

END OF PLAY

About the Playwright

ERIK PATTERSON is an award-winning playwright, screenwriter, and writing teacher.

His play, *One of the Nice Ones*, earned the Los Angeles Drama Critics Circle Award. His theater work has been produced or developed by Playwrights' Arena, the Los Angeles Theatre Centre, Theatre of NOTE, the Evidence Room, The Actors' Gang, the Echo Theater Company, the Lark Play Development Center, Moving Arts, Black Dahlia, Naked Angels, the Mark Taper Forum, and New Group. His plays have been nominated for the Ovation Award, the Stage Raw Award, the LA Weekly Award, and the GLAAD Media Award.

His writing for TV has been recognized with the Humanitas Prize and the Writer's Guild Award, as well as two Emmy nominations. Along with his writing partner, Jessica Scott, Erik has written films for Warner Bros., Universal, 20th Century Fox, Disney, Freeform, MTV, Paramount, Hallmark, and Syfy, among others. Film and TV credits include: *Abandoned* (starring Emma Roberts and Michael Shannon), *R.L. Stine's The Haunting Hour*, *Another Cinderella Story* (starring Selena Gomez and Jane Lynch), *Deep Blue Sea 2*, *Radio Rebel*, and many more.

Erik is a graduate of Occidental College and the British American Drama Academy. He hosts a gently-guided writing sprint online called "Sunday Sprints" that attracts writers seeking community and inspiration to do their best work.

www.erikpatterson.org

Plays by Erik Patterson

Tonseisha
drama / 1 female, 5 male / 45 minutes, no intermission
A young Japanese woman is haunted by the loss of two men: her father, whom she barely knew, and cult novelist Richard Brautigan, whom she never met. Akiko plays out her father/Richard Brautigan fantasies with a new man nearly every night. Each one of her relationships begins in a bar and ends in a bedroom, and she's never satisfied. She's so lost...can she ever be found?

Yellow Flesh / Alabaster Rose
dark comedy / 5 female, 4 male / full length, one intermission
Elliot is lost in a world of sex workers—late night house calls from hustlers and phone calls with call girls. Becky is torn between two worlds—her day job as a stripper and being a mom to fifteen-year-old Rose (a Goth girl who wants nothing to do with her). And then there's Little B, who has stripped away every piece of herself until all she has left is her obsession with Icelandic pop singer Bjork. This troubled family's shared past holds unspeakable horrors and they must join forces if they ever want to heal. *Winner of the Backstage West Garland Award for Best Playwriting.*

Red Light, Green Light
drama / 6 female, 7 male / full length, one intermission
A gay clown. Two lesbian strippers. A pregnant Goth teen. A deadbeat dad. A horny mother. And a girl who thinks she's Bjork. In this stand-alone sequel to *Yellow Flesh / Alabaster Rose*, the Silverstein family journey towards healing is abruptly halted when Elliot becomes the victim of a brutal gay bashing.

He Asked For It
drama / 1 female, 6 male / full length, one intermission
It's the early 2000s, before PrEP. Ted is new to Los Angeles, and newly out of the closet. He goes on a journey through Hollywood back rooms, nightclub bathrooms, and Internet chat rooms—where he meets and falls in love with Henry. But Henry doesn't yet know how to navigate the dating landscape with his new HIV diagnosis, so he breaks things off with Ted...who then makes a desperate decision to win Henry back. *He Asked For It* asks how far are you willing to go for love? And how much will you forgive? *GLAAD Media Award nominee for Outstanding Los Angeles Theater.*

Sick
dramedy / 3 female, 3 male, 1 child / full length, no intermission

David needs to get laid, Gary could use a drink, and Tim would like you to take your top off. Carla craves cocaine, Jeannie's got God, and Pamela keeps digging herself deeper into the funny and frightening world of hypochondria. But when one of their own gets sick for real, they're all going to have to face their greatest fears and grow up.

I Wanna Hold Your Hand
dramedy / 3 female, 3 male / full length, no intermission

Our lives can change in an instant. One moment you're getting engaged, and a few surreal moments later you're sitting with strangers in an ICU waiting room, praying your fiancé will survive a brain aneurysm. While waiting for Frank to wake from a coma, Ada meets Julia, Paul, and Josh, who are waiting for their mom to wake up. A tenuous friendship is born. *I Wanna Hold Your Hand* looks at life, death, and recovery, and what it means to try your hand at living again...

One of the Nice Ones
dark comedy / 2 female, 2 male / 90 minutes, no intermission

A paraplegic woman plays outrageous power games to get something she desperately wants in this dark, twisty, sexy play that takes office politics to new extremes. *Winner of the Los Angeles Drama Critics Circle Award for Best Playwriting.*

Handjob
dark comedy / 2 female, 4 male / 90 minutes, no intermission

An encounter between a white, gay playwright and his black, straight "shirtless maid" goes disastrously wrong when signals are misinterpreted, lines crossed. *Handjob* explores the aftermath of their meeting, as it reveals deep layers of discrimination, discord, and discontent among people who should be allies. How do you know when you've gone too far if you completely ignore other people's boundaries?

Books by Erik Patterson

Pop Prompts: 200 Writing Prompts Inspired by Popular Music
Available in paperback and e-book

Pop Prompts is a collection of writing prompts that will help you dig deeper and break through creative blocks. Each prompt is paired with a pop song. Let the music be your muse as you work on your memoir, novel, script, poem—or even your own songs. This book can also be a daily jumpstart for therapeutic journaling. Use it however you want, whenever you want. As long as you're writing you're doing it right.

Pop Prompts For Swifties: 99 Writing Prompts
Available in paperback and e-book

Every writing prompt in this book is paired with one of Taylor's songs from the first "era" of her storytelling journey, from her debut album *Taylor Swift* (2006), to *Fearless* (2008), to *Speak Now* (2010), to *Red* (2012), and all the way through *1989* (2014). You don't even have to be a Swiftie—anyone can use these prompts for self-expression and reflection. As a bonus, each prompt includes blank journal pages. Inspiration is only a song away. Put on your favorite Taylor Swift album, pick a prompt, and start writing! Taylor Swift has no involvement in this book. The use of her name is merely descriptive and should not be interpreted as a sign of endorsement.

SUNDAY SPRINTS

Need some motivation?

Do you work better when someone is holding you accountable?

Come to SUNDAY SPRINTS.

Erik Patterson hosts gently-guided writing sprints on Zoom every Wednesday from 6 to 8 p.m. PST and every Sunday from noon to 2 p.m. PST. (Yes, it's called Sunday Sprints on Wednesdays because... why not?)

Here's how it works: I give a new writing prompt every fifteen minutes. You write. That's it.

All sprinters stay on mute. Alone but not alone, you can draw creative energy from the community of writers on your screen. This is a fun, low-pressure environment—a safe space for you to experiment with your writing. No worries: I will never ask you to share your work.

You decide how to use this distraction-free writing time. Work on that screenplay, novel, short story, play, poem, song. Do some therapeutic journaling. Write letters to loved ones. Do some technical writing. Create a D&D campaign. Finish your homework. Seriously, whatever you need to work on.

Let's get that writing done. Together.

Join the Sunday Sprints Patreon at:
www.patreon.com/erikpatterson

Subscribe to the Sunday Sprints mailing list at:
www.erikpatterson.org/sundaysprints

www.ingramcontent.com/pod-product-compliance
Lightning Source LLC
Chambersburg PA
CBHW072054110526
44590CB00018B/3167